Dreadful Errors In Judgment

The Wild Worldwide Stories of
Native Florida Outdoorsman
Carl "Sandy" Dann, III

Title:
Dreadful Errors in Judgement
The Wild Worldwide Stories
of Native Florida Outdoorsman
Carl "Sandy" Dann, III

Published by:
Cutting Edge Communications, Inc.
P.O. Box 476, Winter Park, FL 32790 USA

2012 Interviews of Sandy Dann by:
Casey Tennyson Swann

Copyright:
2012 Cutting Edge Communications, Inc.

Printed in USA

International Standard Book Number
ISBN number 978-0-615-75560-1

Other books about Carl "Sandy" Dann, III:
Sandy and Sheila Dann were honored in a book commissioned in 2012 by their partners in a ranch as a surprise gift to them titled *The Hunt For Nirvana, The Gentlemen Ranchers of El Saladero, Uruguay, A Collection of Stories and Images from 2004 to 2011*.

INTRODUCTION

THE GIST: I have a long list of dreadful errors in judgment. How I lived through them, nobody knows. It just wasn't my time. I have been bitten by everything including fish, barracudas, snakes, black widow spiders, and this and that. I grew up in Orlando and have hunted and fished all over the world. I hunted in Mongolia, Pakistan, Canada, North America, South America, and over 15 times in Africa. I went to the Nile basin where the natives had never seen a white person and they wanted to kill us. I've been sailing all over the world. The fear left me somewhere along the line. I've done a lot of stupid things. I had a lot of close calls. There were a hundred times when I should have died. But the stories are usually funny. And I'm still here to tell the stories and laugh with my friends about all of our dreadful errors in judgment.

George Delay   Bob Crieg   Tom Sawyer   Stu Gilman   Myself

Sandy Dann boated and fished summers back from prep school in Florida with friends such as George Delay, Bob Crieg, Tom Sawyer, Stu Gilman and Sandy Dann heading the boat.

CONTENTS

INTRODUCTION

CHAPTERS

SECTION 1:
CARL "SANDY" DANN, III, BORN 1932, FAMILY HISTORY

Sandy's outdoor hunting and fishing adventures growing up in Orlando fueled a lifelong love of the outdoors and exotic animal explorations worldwide. Left an African safari and right a sketch by Sandy in his childhood photo album.

SECTION 2:
SANDY DANN ADVENTURES, A NUMBER OF ERRORS IN
JUDGEMENT BUT HIS NUMBER WASN'T UP YET

SECTION 3:
SANDY DANN'S LEGACY OF ADVERTURE STORIES
AS TOLD THROUGH OTHERS

SECTION 4:
A COLLECTION OF PHOTOS AND SMILES

1924
Developer
Carl Dann, Sr.
at his home
on Hillcrest St.
He was born in
1885 and opened
Dubsdread in 1924.

Carl Dann, Jr., Cathryn Dann (mother), Joanie Dann (sister),
Grandmother Louise, Sandy Dann

SECTION 1:
CARL "SANDY" DANN, III, BORN 1932, FAMILY HISTORY

CHAPTER 1, THE DANNS ON SANDY'S FATHER'S SIDE

My story starts with a conflict in the way of life of two Old-Florida families, highlighted by the two grandfathers and how they influenced me. Grandfather Lawson, on my mother's side, was an affluent, educated Virginia attorney who lived in three piece suits. He was an inventor who built the cable car, and started the two-party political system in Florida by running for congress on the Republican ticket. He sent my mother to study in Switzerland; he was a great believer in education.

In contrast, my father went to Rollins College in Orlando, (Winter Park,) but his father didn't believe in education. Both grandfathers were successful but had two different ways of life. My grandfather Dann was a cracker and developed golf courses and major developments in Florida. He taught me, "Why go to school when you can make so much money without school?"

I grew up in Florida when it was barren. We built canoes and made tree houses. We did so many little fun things just being kids. I loved my childhood in Florida. It was truly the best of times.

This is the story of my childhood with my family here in Florida, and my adulthood with outdoor adventures all over the world. There are so many stories to tell, these are just a few of the memories of enjoying hunting and fishing and having fun.

Sandy's grandfather Carl Dann, Sr.
was a significant developer in
Central Florida. At right, Sandy's
parents with his sister Joanie
at her wedding.

Carl "Sandy" Dann, III
grew up in Orlando under the
influence of his two grandfathers.
He was a wrestler and an avid
outdoorsman.

In 1936 Carl "Sandy" Dann, III, Carl Dann, Jr. and Carl Dann, Sr. at Dubsdread golf course hitting balls. Sandy's grandfather Dann built the second course in Orlando, historic Dubsdread Golf Course. Orlando Country Club was the first.

DEVELOPER CARL DANN, SR.

My grandfather on my father's side, grandfather Dann, built 62 developments in Orange County. He built the second and third golf courses. He is the biggest developer to date in Central Florida. Nobody else even comes half way. If you stand at the corner of Orange and Central Avenues in downtown Orlando and turn around in a circle, every six degrees you will see one of his developments.

Among them were two golf courses, Dubsdread was the first one he built. Dubsdread was the second golf course in Orlando and owned by my family for 60 years before we sold it to the city of Orlando. Orlando Country Club was the first and a few miles away.

The third golf course in Orlando was built by grandfather Dann in Mt. Plymouth, with a 60 room hotel and a 6 mile paved road to nowhere. Understand that not many people were here before World War II. There were three runways for airplanes to land and a tower from which Al Capone's bodyguards kept watch. Al Capone put up money to build the course. They planned for three golf courses with different types of fairways but ultimately it collapsed because of the depression.

Grandfather Dann had a first to fourth grade education. His dad died when he was in the first grade. As a child, he had a goat route to help feed his sister. The Dann family had a land grant from the U.S. government. All Danns in America are from the same family tree in Scotland, and immigrated to the States. As best as we can figure, they left the old country of their own free will and under no duress.

Grandmother Dann married my grandfather when she was 16-years-old. She had just moved to Florida and was right off the train from Atlanta. Her name was Louise and we called her "Weeze." We still have two plants here at the Greens Ave. home that she brought with her from Atlanta.

She didn't drink alcohol. One time she asked, "So, what is in those martinis?" So, I made her one and we sat out on the porch with two of the darkies and they told me all the tales of all of Orlando. Since the help worked in all the homes, they knew all the stories about all of the original families. Like all communities, large or small, there was a dark underbelly that was known of but rarely spoken of openly. Orlando was a rough town. The uneducated crackers had conflicts with the educated landowners, and they all had guns. The business owners all had enemies. They would burn down buildings, and shoot people, and rape people. It was a wild place here.

Before the Civil War, where Orlando is now was then Mosquito County. There were 100 people between what is now Jacksonville and Miami. The U.S. land grant given to my family a few generations back was on Lake Apopka overlooking a hill. It is now a checkerboard of developments.

He was a developer and a humorous motivational speaker and gave lectures all over. He was a total character with Will Rogers type humor. For example, he made a family crest which is in his book published in 1929, *Vicissitudes and Casathrophics*. The crest has a Florida jackass, a Florida boar, the signs he used for his real estate company, a Florida longhorn and a Latin saying that translates to, "No cow shit." He was hysterical.

H. Carl Dann

The Dann family shield in Carl Dann, Sr.'s book *Vicissitudes and Casathrophics*.

6

He died at 52-years-old when I was in second grade. He'd take me out of school to hunker with the crackers. That's where you don't sit on the ground, but you hunker with crackers to hear stories about survival in wild Florida. I missed most of first grade and three months of second grade, because he didn't believe in school and would come pick me up and take me out to teach me about life. There was a big conflict about that with my mother's side of the family.

There were thick mosquitos on the coast in the marshes at that time. People couldn't tolerate to live on the coast till they opened the waterways and the marshes so the water could flow in and out. The mosquitos breed in stagnant water and the marshes gave plenty of breeding ground.

Florida was one of the forgotten states before World War II. It didn't have a medical or dental school in the state, because no window screens or air conditioning, so good reasons. If you couldn't keep the mosquitos out, nobody wanted to live here. To have transportation and housing and the foundations of a community, people would have to want to be here. It's hard to picture that now, with Florida being one of the most desirable places to live.

At that time, a cracker house would have to have 100 to 150 feet around the house of sand, with no grass or trees. The reason is the mosquitos have to have something to hang on to. There were no screens at the time. The first screens were big at first so the mosquitos and sand flies just came through. Can you imagine not having screens, and, of course, no air conditioning at the time?

GRANDFATHER DANN'S BUILDING STYLE WITH ARCHITECT / ARTIST SAM STOLTZ

Sam Stoltz was the artist and architect for my father's buildings including the family home on Greens Ave. off Par Ave., to the south across from Dubsdread.

You can see the artistic detailing of the Sam Stoltz style in the wildlife images integrated in the hand hewn wrought iron banister on the steps going into the guest room, and into metal lamps and light fixtures.

Stained glass features and hand blown glass and etched fish in the tiles in the bathroom layer the artistic detailing. The artistic expression of Florida wildlife flows through the home.

The signature high ceilings of pecky cypress and several ornate stone fireplaces are throughout the house. The master bedroom fireplace has an intricately carved wood relief of wildlife.

The original two bedroom house, still has the original kitchen. A separate bedroom was built on during World War II for officers to live who were stationed in Orlando. The porch leading to the guest room was enclosed to make a dining room. The garage is where the staff lived. A large library filled with books, and a family room complete the home, all still in perfectly maintained condition. Everybody in town helped house the service men who came to train for the Air Force.

A center piece in the guest room is a signed Sam Stoltz original painting signed, "To Carl Dann the miser."

A signed Sam Stoltz original painting signed, "To Carl Dann the miser," is one of the historical artifacts in the Dann home.

Sandy's living room was completely filled with trophies before 42 went to a museum outside of Atlanta. The Dann family home is still adorned with momentos and memories from world travels.

The Dann family home on Greens Ave. sits across from Dubsdread Golf Course in Orlando where Sandy grew up and still lives. Every detail of the home tells a tale as interesting as the man who lives there.

CHAPTER 2, THE MAN IN THE THREE-PIECE SUIT

My mother's father was an attorney gentleman. My grandfather William Claiborne Lawson was the youngest person to pass the Bar, at 19-years-old. He was brilliant. He worked at the patent office in Washington. He invented a system to get iron ore out of mountains using a cable car. He later invented a chair lift for snow skiing which was first used in Stow, Vermont. He patented 15 other things.

He developed the land at Orange and Central Avenues in Orlando, 20 blocks east to Lake Lawsona, which is now a park in downtown Orlando. My grandmother Lawson owned that half acre, which had good soil. On Saturdays, I'd go collect rent in that neighborhood. It cost 50 cents a week to live there at the time.

They bought Stone Island on a lake across from Sanford. They built a causeway to get to the island. Then they built a 9 bedroom, 9 bath house with a pool and a 9 hole golf course. They had two big grand pianos in the living room. They had a huge 30 foot high aviary with exotic birds of the world. They had a black staff of 15 people.

I would stay with them in the summer. Sometimes there were Florida panthers on the island and the panthers would walk on the road because they have tender feet. Sometimes we would see them when we would have to bring a tractor to pull out the Cadillac when it got stuck on the dirt road.

During the depression, they lost all their money. My grandfather had a partner he trusted and he robbed him blind. So, now they had to be practical. The golf course became a cow pasture. The pool was set up to raise fish. The aviary became a chicken coop.

The house is still there and renovated as a clubhouse, and 300 homes are built on the island now.

POLITICS, GRANDFATHER LAWSON STARTED THE TWO PARTY SYSTEM IN FLORIDA

At the time, there was only the Democratic Party, so he ran for office as a Republican, so there would be a two party system in Florida. He ran for Congress with his own money. He didn't win, but he did start the two party political system. People referred to him as "Senator."

He wrote a book entitled *The Quest for Self-Government* and I have one of the last copies.

I never saw him in anything other than a three piece suit, even in the extreme heat of Florida. He lived to be 96.

My grandmother lived to be 94. She was a survivor, too. Having passed 80 years now, I guess I got the longevity genes, too.

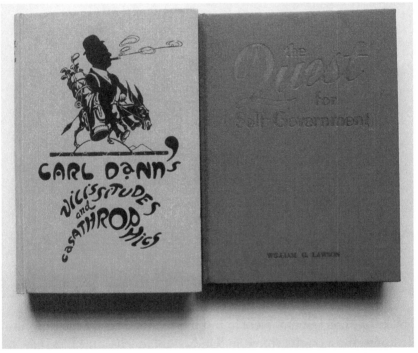

Sandy's grandfather Carl Dann wrote the humorous *Vicissitudes and Casathropics* in 1939 and his more serious grandfather William Claiborne Lawson wrote *The Quest for Self-Government* in 1941. Sandy was influenced greatly by both grandfathers.

Cathryn Lawson was my mother. She went to school in Orlando then Switzerland.

Her sister Elsie Lawson married the composer Rudolph Friml. She was stunning and a beautiful actress. She was roommates with Helen Hayes in New York City and they did three plays together. She travelled to England and France and all over Europe. They were dining together at Tour d' Argent when Lindberg landed at the Paris Airfield LeBourget in 1927. My mother had many stories and adventures from travelling with her sister in Europe.

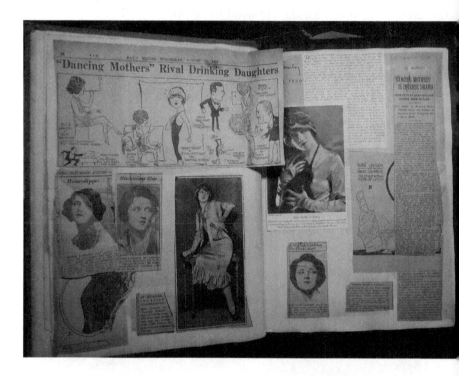

Stacks of photo albums were found in the Stone Island historic family home and now are stored in Sandy's home. His aunt Elsie Lawson, as shown here, portrayed the gold-digger in "Dancing Mothers" at the Booth Theater in NYC. Her roommate, Helen Hayes, played the ritzy flapper.

Sandy remembers his grandparents on his mother's side always in formal attire as shown here with his aunt Elsie.

Sandy's mother Cathryn is shown here at the horse stables that were a part of Dubsdread Country Club.

CHAPTER 3,
FATHER'S ADVICE ON GOLF VS. MEDICAL SCHOOL

I always wanted to be a doctor as opposed to a golfer like my father. The top money winner might make $26,000. The only way pro golfers could make money at that time was through gambling. They would come here to Orlando on the golf circuit back then which was only nine-months a year. In December to February, they came to Dubsdread because it was cold up north. They came to gamble. Some of them were really bad guys, but they were nice to us, and good to me.

I asked my father if I could learn to play golf. He told me that after school, I would come to Dubsdread and practice with the golf pros. Then he would work with me. Then I would play 18 holes before dark everyday, and on weekends, I would play 36 holes a day.

I said, "Dad, when would I have time to hunt and fish and play with my buddies?"

He said, "You won't have time."

I said, "I don't want that."

He said, "Good," and he walked off.

Sandy's sister Joanie won the State Amateur Championship and played with the women pros in professional women's golf.

My father was a five time State Amateur Champion, a three time National Club Champion, Southern American Champion and runner-up twice. He was considered to be one of the best golfers in America.

Bok Tower sits on 4,000 acres at the highest point in the state. There is a golf course there surrounded by three beautiful lakes, a hotel and about 150 of the most enormous mansions. There are about 75 policemen on the property. There are no photos taken, no articles written about it, no apparent way in. It's very exclusive and private. These were the old money people who moved out of Palm Beach when the new money people moved to Palm Beach.

There was only one amateur tournament ever played there. The Walker Cup Amateur teams from America and Britain were invited to play.

My father had just married my mother and drove in to the tournament in a Model A Ford with a rumble seat, and was staying with the president of GM. Upon arriving, my father the jokester, with a servant greeting him asking him, "What would you like for breakfast, Sir?"

My father requested, "Caviar and fresh sardines if possible."

The servant responded, "Would 20 minutes on the patio be sufficient?"

There was a beautiful Cadillac convertible with ribbons tied all over it in the driveway. My father knew this was for first place and Bobby Jones, the greatest golfer of all time, was playing in the tournament against him. Bobby Jones won all four of the major amateur championships to become the greatest golfer that ever lived, then he went to law school and never became a pro. Well, my father wanted that Cadillac, so he won, but the Cadillac with all the ribbons was second prize. Everyone thought Bobby Jones would win, so the Cadillac was the second prize.

My father got this silver bowl, etched with the engraving, "Mountain Lake Club 1937, Invitational Tournament Championship, First Prize Won By Carl Dann, Jr."

My dad was a golfer and a gambler. This one he lost.

Sandy's dad was a golfer and a gambler according to Sandy.

CHAPTER 4,
PRINCETON SCHOOL, PREP SCHOOL, AND IVY LEAGUE

Having a father who owned a golf course with a swimming pool, needless to say, my buddies at Princeton School thought I was fun. The grammar school still exists in College Park in Orlando and has recently been renovated.

One of my classmates was Bob Young, and his brother John Young was a year older than us. He was the ninth astronaut to walk on the moon. I didn't know him well. He was a loner who became one of the most famous people in the world.

Interesting enough, my first year of class, as a first grader, there were four seats at each table. One of the students became my first wife and the mother of four of my children, Nancy Burcham. My wife died young of cancer. If ever there was an example of the good dying young, it was Nancy.

The other two students were Ara May Hishcock and Ray Lilly. We all stayed friends throughout our lives. I graduated from Memorial, there were only two Junior High Schools at the time, Memorial and Cherokee, then I got sent away to prep school. My three friends that I started out with in first grade were number one, two, and three in their class in Junior High.

They were all bigger than I was. I had some diseases early-on which is why my arms and legs are shorter than they should be for my body. I should be six-feet-tall. If you look at photos of my father, that is how tall I should have been. At six and seven years of age, I ceased to grow. I had infantile paralysis. It caused me to miss three months of school in second grade. I had a friend in Atlanta who died from it at that time.

As a child, I was fascinated with medicine. I was always dissecting critters as part of my nature adventures. Two of my parents' closest friends were physicians, so on weekends, I'd work in hospitals and in operating rooms as the clean up boy. So, the die was cast for my desire to be a physician.

Spearfishing
childhood friends
Ted Eidson,
Stu Gilman,
Sandy Dann

INFLUENCE OF IVY-LEAGUE MILITARY PILOTS

At that time, Florida had no medical school, or anything close to it during World War II.

My mother was fascinated with the New England upper class who were stationed here during the war. Their demeanor and activities were always gentlemanly. We were a cracker state and a cracker town at that time. These guys were Ivy League educated and the top Air Force pilots. There was a 60 percent mortality rate in their flight missions over Europe. They would fly the big B17s to England, then on to Europe on bombing runs. These were all Harvard, Princeton and Yale grads and they knew how to fly already. The brilliant people were sacrificed first. The pilots were the best in the country and the navigators had to watch and keep perfect time in order to bomb their exact marks. They were the best of the best.

They were stationed in Orlando and Dubsdread was their officer's club. They had big going away parties there every few months. When they left the Air Force Base in Orlando, they would fly low over the club to say goodbye. Sometimes the tops of the big trees would be clipped and you would see the leaves all over the ground.

I would wake up when they would leave. You would hear the engines. Remember there was no air conditioning then, so the windows were open.

In the two bedroom family home by Dubsdread, my grandmother added a room for the officers training here. There was not enough room in the barracks. And this is what I found, an antique Rolex watch.

This is one of the first Rolex watches ever made. The very first was made in 1905. I sent it to Rolex and they confirmed it was original and said there are no parts for it. In 1940 when it was made, it was worth $30. I had it appraised, it's priceless now. The most expensive Rolex to date is worth $480,000.

I found it in 2007 in a high closet in the room where the officers stayed.

During the war, to feed the officers at Dubsdread, we had 50 acres where we raised crops. We also raised chickens and pigeons. I had to wring their necks sometimes. I didn't like that but they were good eating.

When the war was over, many people had fallen in love with Orlando from their time here, so some of the military people moved back here. They wanted to retire and play golf and the town exploded after World War II. Martin Marietta moved its' military and space engineering here, which brought educated people. The boom started and hasn't stopped. It slows during the inevitable busts that always follow our booms, as in any economy.

As time passed, my mother got together with two of the family doctor buddies and my grandmother Louise, and a half dozen of the prep school people who had been stationed here, and they convinced my father that if I was going to be a physician, I would have to leave the state and go to prep school. In 1947, I was off to Choate in Wallingford, Connecticut.

On my entrance exams, I passed English by one point, math and otherwise I had a 40 average score. I never did learn to write and spell well. After struggling two years at Choate in remedial classes, I finally caught up with the preppies. They had all been in private school all their lives.

Hendrick Smith was my suite mate in tenth grade in prep school. He later wrote the book *The Russians*, which becomes an important detail in one of my later adventures in Russia. He was the bureau chief of the *New York Times* in Russia for eight years.

The first year, tenth grade, I had to take twice to catch up. I graduated Cum Laude, one of the top ten-percent in my class. It was competitive. These were not tacky people; ninety-percent had scholarships to Harvard, Princeton and Yale. The study halls were filled six days a week, then sports. You had five hours a week off on Sundays. Those study habits pay off. When I go back to reunions, 40 percent of my classmates are the heads of major companies.

One guy was the crew team coxswain. He's the guy who says, "Stroke, stroke, stroke," and sets the pace. Crew is a big sport in the Northeast. You get the littlest, skinniest guy, so you chose the guy who is 110-pounds and five-foot-two-inches. When I went back to a reunion, there was a big guy speaking on stage. It was him now six-foot-four-inches; he grew a foot after prep school. His family owned the *Farmer's Almanac*, which has 4 million copies in print in

48 translated languages. They hire the eight guys who are the best in the world at predicting weather. Mistakes? Yes, the worst was in 1884, there was a mistake in the printing office. They misinterpreted and reversed January for July, so it read, "It will snow in New England every day in July." Krakatoa in the Dutch West Indies blew up that year so it did snow in July! For two years, smoke covered the world from that volcanic eruption. The island was one-and-a-quarter miles high and the water under it was one-and-a-half-mile deep and it all blew up in one big puff. It killed tens of thousands of people and affected the world. That was an error in judgment for that guy's family, but it turned out fine. He was a neat guy.

CHAPTER 5,
COLLEGE AND MED SCHOOL: CHAPEL HILL IS WHERE?

COLLEGE TESTING BY GOVERNMENT

After graduation from prep school came, everyone was being tested to go to war. In 1951, during the Korean War, you were either in school or in the service. Remember, at this time, we didn't have computers like we do today. Computers were big and bulky the size of an average house like this house and had little functionality. The government was testing all over the land for materials that would give them concepts of prediction. They were going around to schools to test for great perception. They would have a stack of papers with quiz questions of every subject, and give you three seconds to look at it and guess the answer to see how many you could get right. The military tested all of the prep school students. They came back to test me again and said, "You have survival instinct. You made the right decision in the three second glance more times than when you were given four minutes to answer the questions."

It's complicated and hard to explain. It's an unusual part of the mind from ancient primitive times where they had to make instant decisions to survive. They kept on with the tests and said, "We'd like you to sign up with the military service to do surveillance and you can go to Chapel Hill."

I said, "But I have a scholarship offered to Yale and Dartmouth and ..."

They said, "No, you will go to Chapel Hill."

I asked, "Where is it?"

I hated not going to Yale. Seven U.S. Presidents went to Yale. There were 133 guys in my graduating class and I would have been with people who knew me personally instead of a place where I didn't know anyone, or even where it was.

Well, Chapel Hill is in North Carolina, and in 1951, I found out it was the communist center of the U.S. *The Daily Worker* was delivered to your doorstep every morning.

Duke University is just ten miles from Chapel Hill and North Carolina State makes a triangle. It's the second biggest brain factory and it's in North Carolina. The whole area was filled with scientists in secret buildings; they were building a research center within the university system.

All the Secret Service guys gathered for a meeting at Duke at a fraternity house. They sent for me to come and asked, "So, how are you doing at Chapel Hill?"

My little smart ass decided to be quiet and polite, and just answer their questions.

I was a wrestler but they looked like professional wrestlers. They had perfect physiques and perfect hair; they looked military. They all looked alike. The Secret Service guys all take on a funky attitude. They don't flash a badge, but why else were they there? They never revealed themselves but one or two guys all lived in all the fraternity houses. I would see them around campus but they didn't go to classes.

I made friends. I had been captain of the wrestling team at Choate, so joined the wrestling team. A few of my fraternity brothers had also gone to prep school in New England and were wrestlers.

I was busy studying because I wanted to move on. I was stupid to take four years of school in three years. I missed a lot of playtime. I took classes dawn till dusk.

Interestingly, when I came back after summer vacation, half the teachers at Chapel Hill were dismissed and *The Daily Worker* was no longer delivered. I'm sure some of them were needlessly let go, but unfortunately, some people were clean and evidently, some were not.

FRATERNITY PLEDGE

I joined Phi Delta Theta fraternity. As a young pledge, a brother told me to get my car. We went to the gas station and filled up the tank. He told me to drive. We went through Pinehurst, then through South Carolina, we ended up in Daytona Beach 500 miles away. He wanted to stay but I had to get back to class. We went out on the beach.

He said, "I always wanted to come here."

Then we got back in the car and I drove all night to get back to go to class. We did a lot of fun things. Jack Kerouc would have felt at home with us.

FRATERNITY BOOK CLUB

In the fraternity, I was friends with a chap who graduated from the University of Miami and was in dental school. He convinced me to join the book club that met every Tuesday at 5 p.m. with five guys who were all from Florida. We made perfect martinis out of sophisticated equipment I had borrowed from the science lab. You got one martini, chatted, then went to dinner. You always wore coats and ties in the fraternity house.

We got bored with our own stories, and we started inviting guests in once a week. We invited friends, and teachers. A year later, the dean of the University of North Carolina summoned me. Needless to say, I was nervous walking into his office, which was half the size of a ball field.

His secretary told me when I asked her why I was summoned, "I think you have a problem. You're in big trouble."

After waiting ten minutes to get to His Majesty's desk, he also affirmed what his secretary said, "Mr. Dann, you are in big trouble."

Shaking, I asked, "What kind of trouble?"

He said, "I have not been invited to your book club."

So, we resolved that. We keep the book club framework alive here in Orlando. We meet at the University Club; not the same fraternity brothers, but the same idea.

GIRLS IN COLLEGE

Girls were not involved. Chapel Hill was a male school at the time. At the big dances, not to worry, the girls all showed up in their fancy dresses.

Some were in the dental school to be dental hygienists. They didn't let girls in to Chapel Hill till their third year of college to make sure they were serious about studying and not just at college looking for husbands. We took ten or eleven of Florida's best looking women to Chapel Hill with us. One was Miss Florida. We took them from FSU and University of Florida. My wife to be came up, too, she was one of them. We grew up with all of them. Who knew they would all look like that in college?

At Chapel Hill, I was the big man on campus because I brought all the pretty girls!

DENTAL SCHOOL IDEA

One classmate from Miami was in dental school. His name was Tom Lasalle.

He said, "You don't want to go to medical school. All you talk about is hunting and fishing all of your life. You can't be a physician and go sailing in Tonga, hunting in Africa, exploring in Mongolia, and all the other things you want to do. Now, you can be a dentist and see your patients and take time off if you schedule it right. Better still, you can be an orthodontist, a good one, and you can see all your patients in one month or six weeks. Carry extra staff and you can be gone for a month. To resolve your travel bug and desire to see and enjoy the whole world, with a salary that will allow you to do it, this is what you need to do."

So, I took his advice and that is what I did.

Chapel Hill is the oldest University in the U.S., not a college, but a university.

We built the best dental school in the U.S. at that time. Chapel Hill started the dental school at that time and recruited the best talent in the world to teach and do medical research. They opened their doors and immediately became the number one dental school in the world. Many of the students became teachers and one started a dental school in Florida and another in Texas. You studied because you were either making your grades or in the service. We students wanted to be in college and not in the military, so we studied.

My friend Ben Barker told the dean at that time, "I want to be dean of this dental school."

The dean said, "Graduate number one in your class. Get a degree in business management. Work for a huge corporation. Then come back and we'll make a deal."

He came back many years later and asked the dean, "Would the head of Kellogg, one of the largest corporations in the world, be sufficient for me now to be dean?"

He became dean and I've visited him over the years. It's a wonderful school. We've stayed friends and travelled together to some great places.

CHAPTER 6,
DR. DANN, THE ORTHODONTIST

PROFESSIONAL / GATOR ORTHODONTIC GROUP

I started a study group here in Florida, which allowed me to go to all of these exotic places and to also feed seven, eight, nine kids, a bunch of little Indians. I could work like crazy and then be gone. I was still working on what Sandy wanted to do. If I was going to go into dangerous remote hunting venues, chances are eventually it would catch up with me. My patients nor my family would never suffer.

So, my idea, how it came to me was, "I'm not a rich little fart so how can I afford to do what I want to do and not risk handicapping my family?"

How to maintain my lifestyle was to start a study club with the very best orthodontists in Florida, which we called the Gator Orthodontic Study Club.

We assembled the best orthodontists in the state. We had the best of the best. Five became Presidents of the Florida Dental Society, four were Presidents of the Southern Dental Society and one was the President of the National Dental Society. We started with nine guys who were interested. We met two or three times a year at each other's offices. We'd also go someplace fun like the Bahamas, Scotland, France and other interesting places.

The plan was to first change all of our wills. Gator Orthodontic Group owned our practices. The group would take over your practice if you died. They would take care of running it until it sold. We knew how to run it and we knew what it was worth. We'd keep the wives and children out of it.

Also, I had people to cover when I was gone. If I was going to Mongolia, I never knew for sure when I would get back, or if I would ever get back. To be comfortable, every two years, the entire group would spend two days at your office learning how you work and where everything was. You had to keep the families out because they have no clue about the business and it would go down the tube. Within six weeks, practices would be gone. Maybe 500 patients are coming to you, but something happens to you, they leave and they aren't coming back. So, with the Gator Orthodontic Group, our investment would be protected until sold. It was greaseless. The very next day, someone would step in and take care of the business. The women were happy. The families were happy. It worked like a charm. We had a hundred people begging to get in. Several people copied our system. It worked perfectly.

SECTION 2: SANDY DANN ADVENTURES, A NUMBER OF ERRORS IN JUDGMENT BUT HIS NUMBER WASN'T UP YET

St. Marks 1952, on the dock with fish with Luther, Calvin, "Mac" (Walter McJordan,) Sandy Dann. Sandy and his childhood friends had many outdoor adventures in their boyhoods, and continued to hunt and fish together throughout their lives.

CHAPTER 7,
SANDY CORNERS 800 POUND GOLIATH GROUPER IN KEY WEST UNDERWATER CAVE

In the eleventh grade, home for summer vacation from prep school, I went with Walter McJordan "Mac" to Key West to spearfish. Mac said you could train your body where you don't need air for a while. He used mind over matter to train his body to function without breath for a while. He later became president of the American Diving Team and could work 100-feet of water free diving.

He arrived at University of Florida his freshman year with plenty of money. His father was the manager of Sears in Orlando. He already was a pilot and has his own airplane. He had his own airboat, that he invented and created. He had his own hunting dogs, and on and on. He decided he didn't need university teaching and that he would go take care of himself. He could do extremely dangerous things that other people wouldn't do. He flew for 40 years to odd countries as a soldier of fortune.

He and his wife now live in Cedar Key. In the early 1800s, the first railroad was in north Florida. From Fernandina to Cedar Key, the merchants would have to take huge sailboats around Florida to get to New Orleans. During the three weeks that would take, the food would be spoiling, so they built a railroad from Northeast Florida to Cedar Key, an island in the Gulf of Mexico, which then could get the fresh foods from the east coast to New Orleans, which was a big city in that day. Cedar Key was aptly named because of the large stand of cedar trees. They were harvested and sent by rail to Fernandina then shipped north to be made into lead pencils.

We were both on the Orlando spearfishing team, The Orlando Otters, and we were invited to a two day spearfishing tournament in Key West where certain fish were cleared to be collected, namely edible fish.

Our team of six was split into partners. Mine was Walter. The day was going beautiful and we had collected and speared a few good fish, when all of a sudden we saw the biggest goliath grouper, what we used to call jewfish before that term became politically incorrect.

I'm not sure why it's incorrect. We were four miles offshore on a reef with an average water depth of 20 to 40 feet free diving. Each pair had a boat following them so the fish could immediately be put in the boat so as not to attract men in gray, a name we used for sharks. Out of the corner of my eye, I saw what appeared to be a piece of the ocean bottom moving, and as I came closer, I realized it was a goliath grouper, an 800 pound goliath grouper! He paid absolutely no attention to us and disappeared under a ledge in 30 feet of water.

So, what do we do? We dive down into the cave with no outlet where it's dark as black ink. I have an idea to close my eyes and let them acclimate to the darkness. With my eyes shut, I can squint and can see clearer by having my eyes adjust to less light. Mac guided me down under the ledge. I looked around and didn't see anything. Then I realized the whole back of the cave was one huge goliath grouper.

So, we go back up and the decision was that I would go down again and we both had triple Arbolets, which is a speargun with a cable on it with three notches. It had a lot of juice. So, I closed my eyes and we go down to both shoot him in the head if possible. Everything worked fine and we pulled the triggers simultaneously, and the next thing I know, I'm being pulled upside down. Due to the extreme water pressure of this goliath grouper pulling me, the mask had come down around my neck. The goliath grouper pulled me some 30 to 40 yards and went around a reef never to be seen again. My 500 pound cable to the speargun had been severed. I went back up for a breath of air finally gasping and getting my mask back on and looking for Walter. I see him floating upside down. So, I do a quick dive to bring him back up to the surface and get him into the boat that was following us, where we brought him back and got him breathing again. He still has giant scars on the back where the giant goliath grouper scraped him against the top of the cave when the fish went charging out of the cave. We both survived and we both kept diving and spearfishing.

CHAPTER 8,
BLACK WIDOW ENDS AN EIGHTH GRADE SWIM

In the eighth grade, my family had a camp next to Big Sand Lake across from the present day convention center complex. This was a pristine lake and a beautiful cabin on the property. The cabin was designed by Sam Stoltz, like our other family homes. The lake was 40 feet deep with crystal clear water that you could drink.

This charming girl in school, a little older than me, said, "Sandy, I'd like to go to your cabin. I have a car and can drive us."

So, we go there and decide to take a swim. This was before I even had any fuzz down there. I go to get my swimsuit, they had jock-straps in them then, and put it on. I jumped and hit the ceiling. It had a black widow spider in it and it bit me. It was God giving me a message that it wasn't the right time or place to learn about sex.

I was incapacitated and swollen for weeks. I still have a scar on the tip of my weenie. But I lived.

CHAPTER 9,
MOCCASIN STRIKE TO FISHING BUSINESS IN 1946

In my childhood here in Orlando, I decided not to do a paper route for money. I was a nature guy and hell-raiser and I'd have to get up at 4 a.m. to fold papers and deliver them for just 50 cents. As just a little whipper-snapper, I decided I would fish and do what I loved and make a few dollars a day and let the other guys make the 50 cents.

I would make striker poles, with hollow bamboo and a hammered spear on the end. I added rubber to the end to make spearguns so I could dive and spear fish. I would catch fish each day. Then I would ride my bike with the fish in my basket and ring my bike bell. Neighbors would buy the fish and I would clean the fresh fish for people and make several dollars. If I had been selling newspapers, I would have made just fifty cents.

One day I was at the estate which now is Harry P. Leu Gardens park. There was a big dock over the lake with a big spring at the tip of the dock where I always fished.

I had a big stringer of fish. I was pulling myself up onto the dock. I was cold and shaking and pulled myself up to get warm. I still had my mask on. Masks in those days were made out of the rubber of car tires and double paned glass.

Mr. Leu had replaced a rotten dock with a new one and left the old one with an eight-inch gap. In the gap, a huge moccasin was coiled up having a snooze. When I pulled up dead level on him, he didn't like it. I knew what he was going to do, and he knew what he was going to do. And he did. When a snake strikes, he hits with the power of a professional boxer. He hit me dead center in the glass of the mask and knocked me six-feet back into the water.

I swam to shore stunned. Before I could get to the house, my eyes swelled shut and I had to use one finger to hold my eyelid open to see. They called someone to come and get me and I had a black and blue face for weeks.

The snake struck out and I won. I was fortunate to survive. That was the last day of my fishing business, though.

That was the last day of Sandy Dann's fishing business, but a new trend for diving and fishing. He created one of the first speargun designs with the help of Bo Randall, an Orlando family freind and the maker of famous hunting instruments Randall Knives.

I still have the first speargun I made and glued all the parts together in the garage. When making spearguns, I would take a piece of hollow bamboo, maybe six inches long. I would attach a rubber grip. At one end of the bamboo, I would attach a circular piece of rubber from an auto tire tube to pull back and propel the spear.

For a spear, I used a two foot long, thin welding rod. At one end of the welding rod, or spear, I would adhere tape to make it smooth so it wouldn't puncture the rubber tube. At the other end there was a hammered tip. I had the spear tips forged specifically for my spearguns from a family here in Orlando, the Randalls who still make Randall Knives, for hunting. The spear tips are attached to the end of the spear with a ten inch braided steel cable.

The tips come off into the fish, then the diver can hold them at the end of the bamboo spear. When predators like sharks or eels want to come up and take the wounded fish, you want to let them have the fish, so keep it away from the diver.

You had to work for the fish. You had to hold your breath, free dive down, get close enough to the fish to spear him, then swim back up with the fish.

After World War II, great divers invented the Aqua Lung, which allowed divers to breathe under water. The French underwater explorer Jacques Cousteau was my inspiration. We made our own tanks out of things they stored gas in. The tanks weighed more than us. We had to send them to Miami, which was the only place to get air in the tanks. With the rustic equipment in the early days of diving, three local boys died while diving. Again, for some reason, I did survive.

CHAPTER 10,
REVENGE OF THE MOCCASIN WITH FOUR BITES IN 1980

I've hunted on Deseret Ranch for over 48 years. It's one of the largest cow ranches in the United States and covers Orange, Osceola, and Brevard Counties. Through the property, there is and old railroad tram, appropriately named Snake Tram. Before World War I, they built railroads through the swamps of Florida to get the native timber out. Where they built up the land for the tram for the train to run on, it created ditches on either side, perfect for us hunters to hide in.

On one hunting afternoon there, my friend was off hunting down the tram. I saw a beautiful eight-point buck, fully mature, and feeding 40-yards from the tram. I proceeded to crawl into the ditch to get a clean bow shot. As I was moving to get my bow into position, it felt like I was lying on barbed wire. At the bottom of the ditch, I had seen pieces of an old barbed wire fence. This is where the dreadful errors in judgment come into play. I was actually lying on a moccasin that bit me four times, leaving eight holes near my kneecap.

I was limber at the time and I immediately got my knee up to my mouth, and sucked on it and spit out the venom for about ten minutes, till I couldn't taste the venom anymore. I didn't get enough out, though. By then I was swelling and screaming for my friend who came running to help.

As an outdoorsman in Florida, snakebites are always a possibility, so I kept a first aid kit in the car. I mixed a dose and gave myself one shot of anti-venom that I had packed. I was hunting that day with a dentist friend's son, Mark Todd, who wasn't yet old enough to have a driver's license. He helped get me to the car, laid me out in the back of the station wagon, and drove 90 miles-per-hour towards the hospital. A highway patrol officer pulled us over and saw me and said, "Follow me." He helped us get to the Kissimmee hospital to the helicopter rescue to the main Orlando hospital. I knew this time I was going to die. I was as close to death there as I had ever been. It was so painful. I had never known such pain.

When I got to the hospital, they wheeled me in and I had the full attention of the emergency staff who was waiting on me to get there. They injected me with four more ten-cc shots of the anti-venom to try to save my leg. They had to give me massive doses to keep the venom out of my organs. They brought in a snakebite expert. Snakebites come in categories like hurricanes; with five you are dead and four is mandatory amputation. I had a four.

Now it's 5 a.m. the next day. My leg swelled up as big as my waist and the skin, muscles and everything tore. The venom spread to my feet all the way to my groin by now. The skin and tissue all split as the leg swelled. My heart was pounding to the point of anaphylactic shock. They brought in a heart specialist to stop a heart attack. They had to inject heart medicine right into the heart. The pain was horrible and excruciating and was killing all the other parts of my body. They finally gave me morphine for the pain.

Normally with snake wounds that severe, there would be mandatory amputation. How would I do all the things I loved to do in the outdoors without my leg? How would I hunt, and dive and fish? With no leg, it would end a whole lot of stuff that I loved to do, so I had to save my leg.

I did save myself, and my leg. I had to keep my leg above my heart for six months though, while the whole lymphatic system in the leg healed. I had to get back to work as an orthodontist at my office, so a friend rigged a cart designed to keep the leg up. The staff would wheel me around to the eight patient chairs to take care of my 1,200 patients a month.

This was the revenge of the moccasins from my childhood strike on the diving mask! He tried to take me out again, but I was still alive.

CHAPTER 11,
BLACK MARLIN, THE ONE THAT GOT AWAY IN PANAMA

I had a horror story with a marlin in 1967. It was in Pinas Bay
Panama, where there is the most famous marlin fishing in the world.
I went to Panama where the canal is and to the south is the worst
jungle world I've ever seen. It's 8,000 feet high and it rains 400 to
600 inches a year. Some 300 miles are impenetrable. I've done 15
trips to Africa and have never seen natives like this, real spearchuck-
ers.

My second wife, Barbara, was one of the top lady fisherman in the
world. On a light 18 pound line, she caught the biggest marlin that
any woman or any man had ever caught at that time. She held the
record for 20 years. We were invited all over to fish in the Caribbean
and Pacific. She was sponsored by sportfishing companies to use
their lines, and they would pay for our transportation and all of our
tackle.

I watched her and I figured out how she did it. I would study movies of her over and over again. To land a big fish, she would keep the pressure on the fish. She would keep the drag on. Most people, when they reel back, they give slack which gives certain fish when you release pressure for the fish to do what the fish wants to do, which is get away. She never moved back and forth. She had a certain stance that worked for her to work fish the way she did. When the pressure is consistent to the maximum of what the line can handle, you are more likely to land a big fish. So, that's how she did it. She was a great angler and hunter.

We didn't have nylon back then. Back then, the lines were bigger and the reels were gigantic. With the poles and lines for 100 to 120 pound line, it would weigh 80 to 90 pounds.

I was out by 5 a.m. to get back by 3 p.m. for a fishing tournament on the last day at Club de Pesca on the Pacific.

The boat was stopped while we were reeling in lines at 3 p.m. I see a dolphin, a 50-pounder, so I drop a line and he takes it. We've had strikes all day. To my surprise, a big black marlin comes up and has taken the line. Now I've got a 600 pound marlin on 12 pound test line and spinning gear and he dives down. It's not only my first black marlin, but will be a world record. He does three dives and all the line goes out three times. He spinned to the spool several times. He comes up and does 42 jumps. He took us right into a thunder-storm, with my arms numb and my back on fire, but I wasn't going to let him go.

We backed the boat down on him for 50 miles, and he's taken us 40 miles out to sea. Now it's 5 p.m. We lost an engine so now we've got one engine and we're running out of fuel. By then, the relief boat from the club found us with fuel, and we fight the fish another ten miles, till midnight.

After a heated battle, the marlin was laying sideways with his fin up. We turn the boat then and go right at him. We grab him and are ready to harpoon him. What happened next? He landed on the line and cut the line. He was the big one that got away. I said good-bye. January 2, 1967 is a day I won't forget. I dreamed about it for months after.

My hands, arms and legs were so swollen from the fight of three storms. I couldn't work for a week. You stand in the back of the boat and wear giant harnesses to help hold on to the rod, and you use your whole body.

You could never re-do the thing. It was a series of dreadful errors in judgment that took us out to sea, but we were found.

I did get the record black marlin, in Pinas Bay. We went back in 1969 and I landed an International Game Fish Association world record on 12 pound test line for a 247 pound black marlin.

Sandy Dann with world record marlin, 247 pound on 12 pound test line in Panama in 1967. Sandy's fishing trophies were often recorded in stacks of Sentinel Star articles in Orlando, and also in national fishing magazines and periodicals.

CHAPTER 12,
MORAY EEL HAS SANDY'S HAND FOR LUNCH

I was vacationing with my seven young kids and was going to teach them to fish and play a game of survival. We were in Florida below Sebastian Inlet, about 20 miles north of Palm Beach. There is a 15 mile section of beach there where the rocks stretch out from the shore into the water, creating a great fishing spot. The area has since been purchased by some people from Miami, who bought the Bok Tower, too.

I was an orthodontist at the time and had two weeks vacation. I was going to take the kids. My wife couldn't go because she was in the hospital for six months for a rare disease she caught while we travelled in Africa. It was horrible. There was nothing to cure it. In Africa, when people caught this disease, they burned their huts. It gets under the nails on your fingers and toes and the nails fall off. She came back to Orlando and stayed in the hospital to get well. That's another story.

So, I took the maid and the seven kids and we went to the Gulf Coast but there was red tide so we moved to the Atlantic side of Florida for our vacation.

I had all the kids lined up on the rocks with rod and reels. I kept re-baiting the kids' hooks and they were getting the hang of it. A few of them caught fish but we didn't have enough for our cook out. The little ones were losing their energy.

I thought I'd help them. I saw the tentacles of a lobster sticking out from under the rocks. I bent down in the two feet deep water and put my hand under the rock and grabbed one lobster and took him to shore. Then I came back and got a second one. The older kids cleaned the lobster while I went back for a third. We had gathered driftwood to make a fire to cook the fish.

So, I got down on the sand on the ocean floor again to get another lobster under the rocks. I reached under there into the home of a giant moray eel. He decided to take my left hand into his mouth and sunk his teeth in my hand. I had already envisioned the possibility this might happen to me one day. I knew a little about the animal's

45

behavior, and knew that if I tried to pull my hand out, he would never release me and I would drown in that shallow water. The water came up just over my knee. I would die right there.

The pain was like holding onto a live electrical cord. He chewed for a while till he decided Sandy Dann's hand was not that good to eat so he let it go. I pulled my hand up and blood was spurting all over. The beachside fish cooking lesson got cut short because I had to go to the hospital to have my own hospital food dinner there.

Shores Colony Motel in Vero Beach was owned by Sandy Dann during the time his children were young. The motel was renovated and by the Dann family and devloped into a premiere Florida fishing destination.

CHAPTER 13,
GOLIATH GROUPER ATTACK ON DAUGHTERS IN VERO BEACH

I was married to Barbara at the time, when we bought the Shores Colony in Vero Beach. It needed work and was run down. It had a nice pool and 300 feet of beach on the water.

BOB MILLER'S

SHORE'S COLONY

RESORT MOTEL

LARGE POOL   OCEAN FRONT ROOMS AND APARTMENTS
INDIVIDUAL AIR CONDITIONING & HEATING

FISHING

BOATING

SWIMMING

GOLFING

4600 Hwy. A1A

VERO BEACH

562-6762

The guy who managed it had a radio show and was quite a fisherman, which is why we were staying there. Hearing it was for sale, I met the owner at 10 a.m. with a couple of martinis and told him I was interested in buying the property.

His response was, "How much money do you have in the bank?"

I told him, "I have $20,000 saved."

And he said, "OK. It's yours. It's mortgaged at $60,000 so borrow $40,000 at six percent interest."

I needed to fix it up. We cleaned up the motel, added air conditioning and made it a big success. We set up quite a fishing destination. We had 13-and-a-half-foot Boston Whalers with double hulls that you could launch right from the dunes into the surf.

My wife at the time, Barbara, caught four world records off there. We could reach the reef offshore halfway between Sebastian Inlet and Jupiter Inlet. You could quickly get to 65 feet of water just 13 miles out, and load your boat with fish in two hours. We had Boston Whalers with two regular fishing seats in the back and the driver stood up. We'd use the well in the back of the boat to keep live bait.

I took three daughters out one early morning, at the crack of sunlight. We went right off the main beautiful beach near a shipwreck that went down in the early 1900s. We could still see the stem and stern at low tide and were 400 yards offshore in 30 feet of water. Earlier the girls each caught 10 to 20 pound mackerels.

We put away the fishing gear for swim gear. It was late summer where the water is clear like the Bahamas. We pulled up on the wreck to take a swim and let the kids look at it. We equipped up and jumped in the water. I looked and saw three big tarpon by the hull. Then I looked and saw three jewfish, or goliath groupers as they are called now, in the 500 pound range. I had my pole gun. I always carry it in the water with me. The three jewfish charge up heading toward the children. They appeared to be coming up to eat the kids. I lunged at and shot the first big boy jewfish then turned back and got the kids in the boat.

I went back down to find the jewfish with another pole gun. He had lodged himself in the wreck with the pole gun. I went back down several times and now he has three spears in him and his gills are flared, so he's not coming out.

I wanted to punish him for scaring me. I couldn't get him out of the wreck so I put an anchor in his jaw and cranked up and backed the boat up and tore his jaw off. I saw three big sharks coming so it was time for me to leave. I took the girls back to shore and went back out to the wreck with some men and diving gear. Nothing was left. The sharks ate it all, even the pole gun was missing.

So, I went back home with a jewfish gone, pole guns gone, but the kids were still alive. Their mothers have never forgiven me for that scare. But it was a fun place for divers and fishermen friends, and especially the kids.

Another time, while staying at our motel, the Shores Colony in Vero Beach, a giant whale shark lifted our whole boat out of the water. The sun was first coming up and our Boston Whaler was totally lifted out of the water, much to my surprise. We were slowly let back down into the water. We were sitting on the back of a whale shark, which is actually a docile fish, and he was surrounded by a huge number of fish. We caught an unbelievable amount of fish following that whale shark. We could barely get the boat to plane due to the amount of fish caught. What made the fishing so good there, was that we were between two inlets, so we could go 12 miles out to sea to the reef, and be back to the motel by 8:30 in the morning with fish. There were many adventures in Vero Beach.

CHAPTER 14,
HUGE HAMMERHEAD CIRCLING THE FAMILY IN BAHAMAS

We were in the Sea of Abaco in the park at Bandito Point. I had double anchored the boat as the current was flowing heavily along the reef in the park. The family was moving with the tide along a 25 foot deep reef. All the family had left to snorkel while I was securing the anchors.

David carried the only speargun for protection, although it's illegal in the park. He dove down to pet a leopard ray; the kids like to go down and ride them. So, he's going down to ride this big ray, and the ray gets spooked and takes off. It gets dark, and all he could see was a black bottom. A monster shark was right over him that looked like a submarine. In the water, objects look magnified 20 percent. The shark was within touching distance of him. He said the hammers were the width of his arm span. That's a big hammerhead.

He goes up, starts screaming, and they all huddle together as the giant hammerhead decided to have lunch on my family. Instead of just passing by, she felt threatened for some reason. She proceeded to circle tightly and move them all from the reef out into deep water, out to sea to kill them.

Brantley was just four-years-old, wearing water wings, and he's thirty now. Sheila and his mother, my oldest daughter Carol, were holding him up out of the water so he wouldn't thrash. Both of them are great swimmers and can free dive to 40 feet of water. They were with my sister Joanie, and my sons David and Carl.

Another son, Brannon, was in the boat with me, and heard the screams and knew something bad was happening. So, I leap back in the 31 foot boat and hit the throttles full bore ripping the anchors out of the reef with considerable damage to the reef and anchors.

When I got to the family, 100 yards away, the boat action moved the shark away. They all literally flew in the boat shaking and screaming.

So, I got them in the boat. I drove a mile away and made them all get back in the water. They were begging not to and crying and put one little toe in at a time. I had to force them to get in the water. After a scare like that, such as if you have a bad experience in an airplane, you have to face your fear to get over it. Needless to say, I didn't know my kids had such a negative vocabulary to describe their dad, and that they so questioned my illegitimacy, but they did get in.

The Bahamians said the hammerhead came there every year for as long as they could remember. The shark would come for three weeks into the sound off Hope Town, at Tilloo Cut, to lay her pups each year. The sharks lay their babies, then they go back out to sea, and the babies are on their own. The hammerhead had attacked other people, so the Bahamians baited her up the next year when she came to lay her pups. They killed her and that's how we know exactly how large she was, over 14 feet. She was big.

I swim with the men in gray, or sharks, all the time. She was laying her pups and being protective. It was just the wrong place at the wrong time. And the horrible part of all of this is that I didn't learn anything, I kept repeating it.

CHAPTER 15,
BARRACUDA IN LOVE IN 1959

Another time, I was east of West End on Grand Bahama Cay. There's a tiny island called Memory Rock with a lighthouse, which is the very first island you hit when coming from Florida. It's where the world record 102 pound barracuda was caught.

First of all, you have to understand that a barracuda has the fastest acceleration of any fish in the world. He can hit 24 miles-per-hour in a distance of 10 inches in seconds. He can catch a nice tuna and it's just dead meat with a clear, precise slice, not jagged at all. His bite is sheer and clean, and with his speed, he makes a dead slice.

Now, the barracuda is also friendly because he has no enemies. After many years of running from barracudas, I decided to make them my friends. So, what I would do with my pole spear is shoot a little grouper or snapper, and hold it out for the barracuda to eat, which he gladly did. After a few feedings, he became my buddy.

Unfortunately, when a barracuda becomes your buddy, he wants to swim next to you. So, now he's between my legs, against my arms, and all over me. It takes a complete psychological change not to move or jump or thrash or kick, and just calmly let the 'cuda rub you good as a thank you.

Some of Sandy's fish trophies adorn the walls of the dining room in the Dann home.

CHAPTER 16,
TYPHOON IN TONGA IN CAVES AND WAVES

I took Malcolm and Jane Kirshenbaum and Kitt Young, a girl I was dating, sailing for my first time in that part of the world for exotic fishing and diving. I had sailed all of my life all over Florida and the islands of the Bahamas. I took my friends to Tonga to sail which is the only island left in the South Pacific that is a kingdom. They have many little volcanic islands filled with jungles. They have no money. They barter.

So, we are on a CSI 44 sailboat for a few weeks. On the third day, we heard on the radio that a giant typhoon was coming and everyone was to take cover. We found an island 400 feet high, the equivalent of a 40 story building, to get behind. The reef on either end of the island was 1200 yards long and 200 yards wide. The outside wall of the island had been hammered by the ocean for centuries creating huge cliffs. The tides there averaged 15 feet. So, on either side of the island, the reefs were smooth with large holes in them.

We put both anchors on shore to secure the boat. The wind blew and the waves hit and a 30 foot tide rose over the reef. We could feel the huge waves hit, the whole island shook.

In the morning after the storm had passed, the natives came out in dugout canoes to grab trapped fish and shells washed from the caves into the reefs.

I climbed to the top of the island to look at the ocean. There was this Australian pine hanging over the cliff. The water from the waves, dug caves and sent the water spewing out of the sides of the mountain in blowholes from years of the water flowing through in storms. I wandered down to the flat area, now at low tide, and found the entrance to the caves. It was the most beautiful thing in the world. There was a series of incredible waterfalls. Over thousands of years, stalagmites hung from the ceiling with water dripping down them, with crabs clinging to them. It was like turning on floodlights to look at the beauty of nature. There were also huge bats, the largest in the world. You could hear the screeching of the loud bats outside of the caves.

The next crevice was bigger and better. There were 300 yards of space inside this mountain. Each room in the cave had different crabs and water spouting down the side and all overlooking the ocean. I was awestruck by the beauty before me.

I screamed down to my friends and said, "You've got to come up and see this!"

They are always suspicious of me and think I'll get them into danger. They did come and peek in, then they bailed out when a big wave hit and they nearly got washed away.

The tide changed and the water started to come in but I wanted to go back to the middle of the island. I had my mask and flippers so decided to stay for one more look. The waves were starting to come in and the tide goes up five feet in an hour. So, I go up higher and higher, nearly 400 yards, till I can't go up any further.

"I'm going to die. This is it," I tell myself if I don't get out quickly and I said a few Hail Marys.

The sun's going down now. I see a log that never moved in the water. So, I put on my mask and flippers and step into the top of a wave to ride it to get to the log. The 50 foot deep water was crystal clear so I could take a deep breath and swim under water to get to the log. As the huge waves rolled through, I could hold on to the stationary log under water, and let the waves roll over me so I wouldn't wash away. I'd hold my breath and hold on to the log over and over again. So, I'm alive.

The tide is falling now and the water will all go out in the next hour.

But now, the waves are crashing on the reef with such force, that I'm still going to die for sure. So, I'll die smashed on the reef in little pieces or the waves will take me out to sea. I noticed every now and then, it was not a 20 foot or 30 foot wave but a 15 foot wave. I kept ducking as the big waves came and had to make a quick decision or be washed out to sea. I've been surfing all of my life and the only way out is to surf a wave. I caught a 15 foot wave to body surf on, because it didn't have enough juice to break but could carry me across the reef, then I'd just have a half-mile swim back to the boat.

As I swam up to the boat at sunset, I could hear them crying and moaning and carrying on. They didn't know how to sail and thought they were stuck and thought I was a goner. It wasn't my time. I'm the luckiest guy on earth. I pulled myself up on the back of the boat and asked, "So, what's for dinner?"

Needless to say, they were a tad bit angry.

CHAPTER 17,
RIDE ON A 75 FOOT WHALE IN TONGA

On a sailing trip with Malcolm and Jane Kirschenbaum and Kitt Young, we had another big adventure, with a beluga whale. We saw this huge whale and decided to get a closer look at her. We followed the whale around and I got in the skiff safety boat or dinghy. We were trying to stay up with the whale and I'm in the little boat hoping to get up close enough to swim up to the whale and see her baby. When the whale surfaced, we could see she was about 75 feet long with her baby calf. I jumped in the water with them and I'm hanging on to the fin of the whale, and, of course, she doesn't know I'm there. She took a few big breaths, and the whale goes up and then dives down and takes me down with her. The water carries me down. Picture a sinking ship and how it sucks things down with it under the water. The next thing I know, I'm 40 feet down with no air. I came up within seconds of passing out. I was fortunate I wasn't floating waiting for a shark to find me.

CHAPTER 18,
WILD MONGOLIAN TRAIN RIDE AND CRAZY PLANE RIDE IN 1975

I was with Malcolm Kirschenbaum, Jim Steinhaus, Craig Linton and Jim Swann. We spent a week in Moscow seeing ballets and going to museums. At that time, Russia was not our friend. Russia is still not really our friend. I had made friends with some of the locals, even if our countries weren't friendly.

In Russia, 3 million members of the communist party controlled 300 million citizens. How does that happen? Food was severely rationed, so to shop for just yourself, would take seven and a half hours a day just to get food to eat. For example, you are a school-teacher. You hear the store down the block has some codfish for sale. You dismiss class to get in the line that is two city blocks long. You finally pay for your purchase of the codfish, only enough for you to eat. Then you wait in another line for two hours to get your codfish. Then you wait in another line to be processed before leaving the store. So, the total average time spent getting one meal, is seven hours. Russia controlled the citizens by controlling the amount of food they could have. The average Russian had a spending power of under $150 to $200 a year.

So, this is the political climate we find in Russia. We found some wonderful, what we called, Bolshoi Girls, who were the black marketers. Through them, we were able to obtain beautiful relics from the time of the czars of Russia, when it was the richest country in the world.

So, the KGB was curious about us and followed us everywhere we went until we proceeded to go on our hunting trip. We headed on the plane to Mongolia. This was my second trip and I was well received. When I heard of other hunters going there between my own trips, I would send goodies to the Nomads. The Mongols, as we called the nomadic Mongolian people, were totally isolated by the Russians out of hatred and fear that came from Genghis Kahn and his four sons in the 1300s. All of Russia was captured by Mongolia, who then ruled Russia for 330 years. When Russia regained power over Mongolia, they were punished severely by total isolation, which obviously affected us as hunters there. We were in total isolation with the entire country. There is no communication at all in Mongolia.

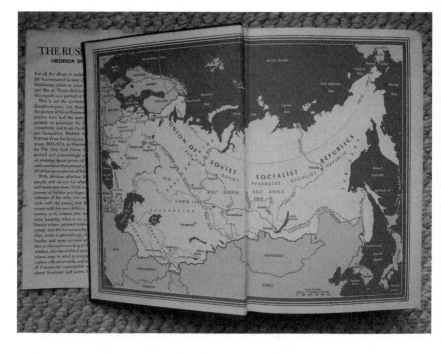

The capitol of Mongolia is Irkutsk. You can see that it is equidistant to fly to Moscow in Russia or to fly across the ocean to the U.S. This geography will help you understand the stories about Russia. If you drill a hole in Orlando you come out the other side of the globe in Irkutsk.

Once we landed in the capitol Irkutsk we were stepping back in ancient times, as these people had no money. They lived off the land. They were totally controlled by the Russians, for example, each person was allowed to own 50 animals. Over 50 percent of the people were still nomadic horsemen.

The appeal for hunters is that quite a few animals live in that part of the world, that only live there. Hunting with the nomads was a wonderful experience, not fully to be understood unless you have actually experienced it yourself.

Fifty percent of the 3 million people in Mongolia were nomads who had to migrate 500 to 1,000 miles a year, when the cold weathers hit that part of the world. The winter temperatures averaged 20 to 40 degrees below zero, if you can imagine. Through the Russians in Canada, that I booked my safaris with, I managed to be able to send gifts in the three months that Mongolia was open to hunting when it wasn't in the bitter cold. The two most popular items they liked were contraceptives and small handheld solar powered calculators to do math. This little $20 item amazed them that it could add and subtract. Remember, there is no such thing there as power or electricity, so to them, this was an amazing gift.

The only problem with Mongols is that they never bathed because where we were there was virtually no water except a few wells and small streams. Because of the scarcity of water and them not being able to bathe, they brushed themselves. It's hard to describe. They would rub themselves down to wipe off the dust of the desert.

Men, women, and children all slept together in large, round tent-like structures, called yurts. The yurts are beautifully designed with roofs with a hole in the top for circulation. The walls of the yurts are two-ply filled with the hair of animals for a 12 inch thick insulation. They are handmade transportable dwellings using a design from 3,000 years ago. Inside they paint many designs and make it beautiful. Living there is as primitive as it gets, which is the charm.

They can fold up their whole camp within an hour, and hook it up to horses and camels, and the whole community can move. Once the game animals have grazed in an area and eaten all the grass, they pack up and move.

This is a stag maurl,
which is like our elk. It's a
1,000-pound brute animal.
There are lots of little sheep.
Notice there are no trees.

The camels are double-humped, not single-humped like in Africa or India. With the two humps, it's easier to sit on them to ride them, but still not comfortable.

The Mongols can stand and ride on a horse for two days straight without getting off of the horse. That is how they conquered the world. "Where is this guy going?" I asked. The guide told me, "He's going for a ride for two or three days and he'll be back."

Instead of a lasso, they have a noose design. They take the long
pole, put the noose around one of the large animals, and can bring
them right to the ground.

Look at the horns on these rams. This is a sheep! But not like the
little sheep we have here in the states.

This is the heart of darkness in Mongolia in the mountains.

This is the edge of the Gobi Desert, the great desert of the world. This is a typical scene with three yurts and the animals living around the site.

Our guide was supposed to speak English but he spoke French, which was close enough.

So, back to the Moscow story, we were being obnoxious, not what guests in a country should be and the Russians were going to give us grief. We end up in Le Metture. We separated to do our hunting. Jim Steinhaus and Craig Linton went on one safari to a new hunting reserve some 600 miles away.

Malcolm Kirschenbaum and myself went as non-hunters with Jim Swann to help him collect his trophies. Jim Swann is Jack Eckerd's son who started Eckerd Drugs.

We finish our hunting three days early, so we elect to take the Trans-Siberian Railroad train through Russia, to Irkutsk, which is 40 miles from Lake Baikal. The lake has one-fifth of all the non-frozen fresh water in the whole world. This is a very interesting contrast to Mongolia that has not much water. Lake Baikal is 65 miles across, 400 miles long and one mile deep. It's freezing cold. It's one of the oldest lakes on Earth, where the earth opened up millions of years ago.

We load up our stags and sheep and trophies on the train to Irkutsk. We then will go to Moscow from there. We stuff one stateroom with all the animals, guns and hunting gear. So, we have another beautiful stateroom, travelling 4,000 miles across the tundra in Russia in this ancient train and the only thing we have to drink, unbeknownst to us, was our 12 bottles of vodka. We thought there would be food served on a dining car on the long train ride. Well, wrong! Thankfully Mongolian vodka is 70 proof and not 100 proof. We had shaved and showered and looked like humans for our three day trip, but still could use a better shower.

We expected to see beautiful scenery and were sadly disappointed to see the same scenery as the Gobi Desert and the flatlands. For two days, it was boring countryside. So, a continuous gin rummy game began. For two-and-a-half days, all we had was the vodka we brought, and water and tea from the steward. We also had two pounds of Beluga caviar, the world's finest.

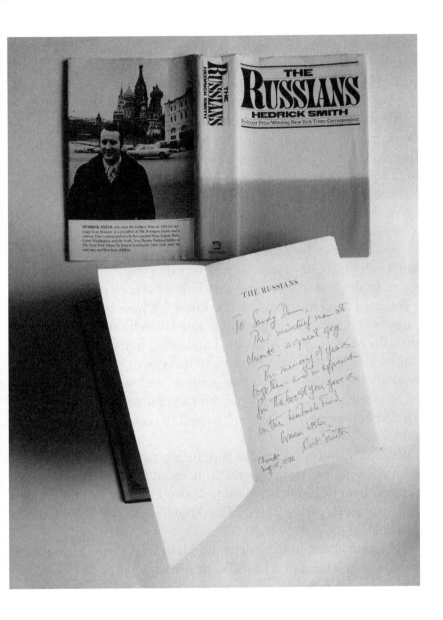

The Russians describes the horrible treatment by the communist party members. A classmate of mine at prep school at Choate, Hendrick Smith, was the author.

A classmate of mine at prep school at Choate, Hendrick Smith, was the Bureau Chief of the *New York Times* for Russia for eight years. He wrote a world famous book, *The Russians*, which described the horrible treatment that was inflicted upon 300 million people by the 3 million communist party members. The book was mandatory reading in many high schools in America at the time. In Russia, however, the book was forbidden under penalty of death, of dismemberment of your body, if the book appeared in Russia anywhere.

Unbeknownst to me, Jim Swann had brought a copy of the book with him; totally forbidden.

Upon arrival at the Russian border, the KGB boarded and investigated every piece of luggage we had very thoroughly. They tore it all apart. In Jim Swann's suitcase, they found the copy of *The Russians*.

The head inspector demanded to know, "Whose book is this?"

Jim Swann took his thumb and pointed directly at Malcolm. With that, the KGB grabbed Malcolm, handcuffed him and left the train.

Immediately there was a lurching in movement of the train car. I went about to examine what was going on and we had been separated from the rest of the train and our train car was put on a siding. The other passengers were removed and the car was sealed; locked shut.

We continued on with vodka and the gin game. I asked Jim, "It's been eight hours. Are you getting concerned for Malcolm? Why did you tell them the book belonged to Malcolm and not to you?

He responded with a laugh, "That little Jew can talk himself out of anything."

Eight hours later, Jim was right and Malcolm returns. Jim doesn't ask where he's been or if he's OK, he just says, "Your deal!" The timing was funny and it was funny that he just said the two words.

I wanted to know the details of his eight hour ordeal and finally heard. Malcolm said they put him through the screws. You have to understand the mindset of the KGB. The Russians had Gulags, or forced labor camps, from the 1930s to 1960s, where Stalin butchered millions of people. The Gulags were a series of open-air prisons in Siberia where many of the prisoners died of the cold, and many more from harsh work conditions. Some were criminals, Jews, and authors were sent there if they wrote derogatory things about Russia. Instead of killing the writers, they would work them to death. The KGB wanted to know if Malcolm was Jewish and where his family came from originally. You know what they did to Jews in Russia; they killed them all. Hence, a big part of the investigation for Malcolm, was when Malcolm's family came to America. He talked himself out of trouble, just like Jim said he would. They hooked us up to the next train, and off we went to Irkutsk. It could have been a close call.

PART TWO, There's more!
The horror story has not ended. We get to Moscow in Russia, then to Irkutsk in Mongolia.
We are in Irkutsk to join our comrades who are furious at us because the government made them pay for us because they said we left without paying our bills at the hotel.
We all now continue heavy drinking and head back to Moscow to catch our plane out of Russia. Before going to the plane, to the most northern coast of Sweden, we were paying our duties, calling the U.S. Embassy, and saying goodbye to our friends. Still smelling rancid, we are waiting to board the plane. I asked the men to lay off the booze as we had a long flight. The next thing I know, they each have a quart of vodka in their vests, which they drank before they got on the plane. Nobody has ever seen on a plane what is about to happen. It was the number one worst behavior ever. I was fussing at them as we stood in line for three hours to get on the plane. In Russia, you stand in line for everything. For three weeks now, we've had no good baths and our hair is dirty. We look like scumbags. We boarded with our animal skins and smelly clothes.
In the line, 50 English women were watching these guys swearing and cussing and carrying on, and a proper English gentleman addressed the men, "Say there, can you watch your language?"
Steinhaus mimics him and his reply is, "Fuck you. By the looks of you, I'd rather not."
After departing, Jim Swann, who looked like Kris Kristofferson

at the time took the stage. He got up and started singing Motown songs and was blaring out, "Heard it through the grapevine..." and he went on and on. He was standing in his seat singing at the top of his lungs for three hours straight. When he first stood up, everyone thought he was a star and rushed towards him. The weight shifted so fast, the plane got out of balance and started dropping. The whole plane could have fallen out of the sky. They had to get all the people in their seats. But not Jim Swann. The authorities had no affect on him.

The rest of the group was playing gin rummy. When Malcolm would lose, he would stand up and throw the cards all over the plane. The pilot came out a few times and told us, "I'm going to throw you in jail." I just knew we'd be locked up.

We landed to refuel the plane and make a quick stop. Two of the guys got out and into the liquor store and got four more quarts of vodka and drank them in eight hours with no food.

We finally land. The guys were totally comatose, finally passed out and now I can't wake them up. There was a woman sitting next to Jim Swann on the whole flight. She stands up, takes her high heel and digs it into his crotch. We got wheelchairs to strap them in to transport through the airport, and stuffed them in taxis. Now we were here in Sweden at the number one hotel, The Grand Hotel across from the palace. We are there to clean up, have wonderful dinners, and then I was going to Paris. I couldn't wake them up at the hotel, but I got together all their documents. They needed another signature. We wheel over Steinhaus to the big sweeping desk with three people behind it. He stands up and leans over against the desk to hold himself up. He was trying to write, but couldn't get himself together. He reached for a candy bowl of sweets, and, remember, he hasn't eaten for days, and he smells it. With that, he throws up all over the lobby desk and passes out on the floor.

We had reserved the best rooms in suites in this Five Star hotel to get cleaned up. I get Malcolm in his room and he's passed out in his bed. Jim Swann is so big that I can't lift him up, so I get him half way up, with his head on the bed with his knees on the floor, and when I checked on him twelve hours later, he hadn't moved.

So, now we are cleaned and shaved and theoretically sobered up. We have reservations at the finest restaurant, Opera Keller, in a Swedish city of about 2 million people. At the table next to us is a couple, and the woman is pointing at us and yelling, "There they are!" She recognized us from the plane fiasco. She was the one sitting next to us. We sent them two bottles of champagne and she finally looks up and toasts us from her table.

You know they thought, "Crazy Americans!" It was a wild plane ride with one catastrophe after another.

CHAPTER 19,
TWO WIVES AND THE KGB IN 1980

Sheila and I were with Jim and Christine Steinhaus on another Russian adventure. We took a tour of Kiev and St. Petersburg, then back to Moscow. We spent a week there before Jim and I went hunting in Mongolia. We had the guns and hunting equipment shipped to Mongolia ahead of time. At that time, no communication existed in Mongolia, but they knew when we would arrive, and it all worked out each time.

In Russia, we were staying in an International Hotel overlooking the Kremlin in the Square. The last night with the girls, we went to a big restaurant that had a big wedding party. We sent the wedding party a fifth of vodka and they sent us a bottle of vodka back. In the meantime, we're up dancing with the girls, and our wives got tipsy. They were not big drinkers.

There was a huge limo at the door when we walked out. Men opened doors for us and we got in. We thought it was a taxi, but it was a KGB limo. They drove us around Le Banca, where they grind people up and flush them into the river. These were the "nasties" of the KGB. We circled the square a few times with the statue of Iron Felix, the ruthless guy who did all the massacres and ran the KGB. After circling several times, they took us to the International Hotel and said, "Leave this country Dr. Dann, and never come back."

All night long they were looking at our room. There was a guy outside in the limo all night, and if I looked out the window, he shook his finger at us.

Jim and I had planned to leave at 3 a.m. to catch the plane to go hunting in Mongolia. So we left as planned unseen by the KGB.

The girls left later that morning but the KGB were waiting for them. Christine, was going to Germany and Sheila was coming home to the U.S. The KGB couldn't decide whom to follow, so they followed Christine to Germany.

It was a great hunting trip after that with no interference from the KGB.

CHAPTER 20,
KOREAN AIR LINE SHOT DOWN, SO STUCK IN MONGOLIA

The next time I was in Russia with Jim Steinhaus, in the height of the Cold War in 1983, a Korean Air Line plane was flying over Russian air bases and got shot down. It was an international flight with a U.S. congressman and other dignitaries aboard. The Korean Air Liner flew over Russia for three-and-a-half hours, where they kept missile bases. The plane was pretending to be lost but really it was not. It was a spy plane loaded with important people. So, the Russians said, "Enough of that!" and shot them down. The U.S. didn't admit it was a spy mission until many years later. It caused Russia to take action against us, meaning that all Embassies from Western cultures in Russia were given just a few days to leave. Britain, France, U.S., all no longer were allowed to have people in their country. We didn't know that the international chaos had started because we had no communication with the outside world. We were on the edge of the Gobi Desert in the hills hunting sheep.

I was hunting on the edge of the Gobi, and there were some people riding horses. I saw a flare. There was a guy in a Russian Jeep who said he had met me at a hunting meeting in California. He asked, "Didn't you know that the Russians are about to declare war against the U.S.?" He was going out through China and was going to have a tough time. The Chinese kept one million people along the border of Russia to keep the Russians out. Those two countries didn't get along.

So, we have to leave our hunt and go back to Moscow, the way we came in. We've got to go five-thousand-miles across Russia with no tickets, no nothing. We know people in Russia because we've been there a lot, so that will help. We take a private plane back to Ulaan Batar. This takes most of our money.

As I have said, there is no communication in Mongolia. Russia cut off Mongolia completely from the rest of the world. Here's a history lesson. Russia and China hate Mongols. From 1180 to 1250 they controlled all of China and Russia and India. Horsemen, under

Genghis Kahn, took over that whole part of the world. They were vicious. They created the curved bow and arrow. They are mobile people who can withstand winters of 20 to 40-degrees below zero. The Mongols would invade and conquer a walled city. They would threaten total destruction should they not submit. They would leave a few Mongols in control and move on. If there was resistance, total death and destruction to all. The Mongol nation of only 3 million people, controlled all of Russia for 330 years. You have to understand the power of these Mongols. If you look at a globe, Mongolia sits between Russia to the North, China to the South, and India to the south of China, and the tough Mongols ruled all of those people. That's impressive. So, we got out of the desert to Ulaan Batar, if you measure from there to Moscow, it's the same distance from our flight into New York from London. Russia is half again that distance. So, think about Orlando to Hawaii, or Orlando to New Mexico, or Orlando to Canada, that is how far we would have to travel. It's a magnificent country. A nice thing about Mongolia is the terrain. I asked, "Where are the roads?" They responded, "We have 12 miles of roads." You don't need roads, you just drive across the desert to wherever you want to go. You think that for three centuries, on horseback, they took over that whole part of the world and did that whole part of the world want to kill them? Yes.

The Mongols liked us because we would bring them things. I'd send gifts, too, with other hunters, such as calculators, contraceptives and antibiotics.

We are living in yurts, or exotic mobile tents, which they packed up and moved with us. We've notified a plane to land in the desert through our interpreter so we can get out of the country and back to the U.S. We don't speak the Mongolian language.

The day before we leave, they put a blindfold on me and lead me up the top of a cliff to watch the sun come up on the edge of the desert. There were maybe ten clouds. Beyond that I could see something moving. There were several hundred horses and cows and camels. All the people I had sent gifts to came to say goodbye. They were a gracious people and appreciated things. They gave me a big goodbye by showing their wealth, which was their animals.

I got into the private plane to Ulaan Batar the capital and asked for the Embassy. There wasn't one so I had to bribe my way out. Two planes went out of there each week, that could hold only 25 people each, so it took all of our money to get out of Mongolia to Moscow.

Then we flew to Russia to Moscow. It's the same distance as flying from England to the U.S. We landed at the International Airport, at the time it was the third largest airport in the world, and there wasn't a plane there. We arrive and we haven't bathed in seven days and we smell like goats.

There is no Embassy. The Russians closed the U.S. and English and all European Embassies.

The Russians average income was only $300 a year, so we could pay $200 for fineries, like carved ivory on a knife or an intricate cane handle that belonged to royalty there. The cane was made of a rhino horn. For this, I gave the Bolshoi girls $200 and they were ecstatic because that was like a year's salary for them.

So, I had business exchanges with this group of Bolshoi girls over the years and called them to help us. They slammed the phone down because they knew they were being monitored. There were guys with machine guns all over the airport. There was nobody to call because the Russians made everyone at the Embassies evacuate.

In the heel of my boot, I had one gold Krugerrand, which is a South African gold coin, for an emergency like this. I had taken the heel off, put in the coin, then nailed the heel back on. I saw one woman behind a booth, maybe the distance of three football fields away in the huge airport. When I got to her, she spoke a little English. She told me the last plane out, a small 100 person plane going to Vienna was filled. I gave her the Krugerrand and asked again, "Do you think you can help us?" She bit the coin to test if it was real and this time she responded, "I think I can help."

Some four hours later she waved to another girl and the girl signaled back. We saw this sloping tunnel with all the people getting on the plane. The plane was taxiing out. This was a problem because we had to cross 3,000 miles. That would be like sitting right here and trying to get to Honolulu.

So, I have to tell Jim, "We are staying here forever incarcerated."

The girl is still signaling so we get our cart of guns and animal skins and walk towards her. The plane stopped 500 yards out on the runway, we walk out and they put another ladder out for us to board the plane. They load our guns and animal skins and we board.

There were two KGB guys in the only first class seats, with briefcases handcuffed to their wrists. The pilot spoke a little English. He made the KGB guys go to the back of the plane and he asked us, "Would caviar and champagne be sufficient for you?"

We went to Vienna. I kissed the ground when I got out of Russia. I kissed American soil, too. I kissed both.

We really smelled. We told the people at the hotel in Vienna what happened to us and they opened up the honeymoon suite for us. When we left, they never even charged us. We took hot baths and shaved and got haircuts and cleaned our clothes. After that, we went to Paris and proceeded to eat great food and drink for a few days. The people on the U.S. mission didn't survive since the Russians shot them down, but Steinhaus and I survived another close call.

Over the years, Sandy traveled to the far corners of the world to hunt and fish with many different friends. Some trips induced extreme fear, some were memorable for just plain fun.

CHAPTER 21,
ONE MORE FORBIDDEN TRIP THROUGH MOSCOW TO HUNT IN KAZAKHSTAN

I was a member of the Safari Club, a national club where we would meet international hunters who go to odd places to hunt. We would meet in the U.S. at San Antonio, Reno, California or other places. At the meetings we booked hunting trips all over the world hunting animals and shooting birds. At the meetings, I met Russians living in Canada who booked the trips to Mongolia.

Through the Safari Club, I was asked by a charming gentleman, a Kazak, to do a hunt in Kazakhstan. It's landlocked in the middle of nowhere in Central Asia and Eastern Europe. Since Kazakhstan declared themselves independent from Russia, they were opening hunting in Kazakhstan. They wanted to see if international hunting could be established there to bring in dollars. I use the term "dollars" because they considered that to be where stability was, as the Russian economy was going down hill at that time.

So, two friends, myself and Chuck Meyers and another friend booked a trip to Russia. Russia, however, had taken away my ability to be in Russia and forbidden me to be in Russia because of previous trips. To get to Kazakhstan, we had to land in Moscow, and be picked up from the Kazakhstan Embassy. We were taken to the Embassy and told we couldn't leave the grounds, which we immediately did do, because we had a three day wait for only two planes a week that flew from Moscow to Kazakhstan. I felt safe with some old friends to show them Moscow.

Kazakhstan is where Kruschev had his summer home, and it was also home to quite a few rare animals that only exist in that part of the world. The ugliest prehistoric animal I've ever seen in my life is there, a saiga. We collected a few to bring back.

We covered 3,000 miles of countryside in four weeks, examining hunting game to see if they could make money. Every place we went, we were unbelievably entertained by the locals. Communicating through a full time interpreter translating all the fantastic stories we could think of about the U.S., the locals couldn't get enough.

They have an untenable language so we would have to have an interpreter. The locals everywhere kept us up till the wee hours of the night telling stories of America and what America was all about. The guide later came to visit America for two months.

In the 3,000 miles we covered in Kazakhstan, we would stop at burned out Russian police stations to relieve ourselves. They used to be guard stations, and now were just sitting there empty.

The hunting starts at a great chain of mountains. Twenty miles out of the capital city, you climb 15,000-feet high to find rare sheep and animals living only in that part of the world, which made hunting great there.

After hunting, sitting in a nice hotel in the capital, we heard English being spoken. We went into the room, and there were 20 people from American and British oil companies negotiating a pipeline. It was interesting because those oil companies knew of the downfall of Russia, but Russia didn't know it yet. The oil companies were so far ahead of our government, too.

We had to fly back out through Moscow in the Kazak plane. We landed and had to go to the local airport next to the international airport.

All of Russia had declared a no-work day that day and all the people were in the field harvesting their own food. The people would not be able to eat unless they harvested their own food. That's when we knew it was over. Russia was finished.

CHAPTER 22,
AFRICA AND ALMOST ONE VERY SHORT MARRIAGE IN 1980

After five years of dating, I married Sheila, and we took a honeymoon trip for a month to Zambia, in the Heart of Darkness in Africa. We were with David Ommoney, one of the greatest hunters. I always seem to run into the best of the best for everything I do. I waited for two years to get to hunt with David the first time. I also brought two friends on the trip, Bob Buonauro and Fred Williams.

We start with a single engine plane ride, not a twin engine, and they will deliver our clothes by Jeep. They start by clearing the animals off the runway. Then they measure off where on the runway the plane has to be airborne to avoid smashing into an eight-story tall tree at the end of the runway. So, they marked where he had to stop, but we weren't airborne and he didn't stop. He kept going and finally at the end of the runway, he bounces up and turns the plane sideways then straight again. None of the instruments work and I ask the African pilot how he is flying the plane and he responds, "I listen to the engines."

On our honeymoon, we are going to catch the last lechwe. It's a small antelope that lives in the water in shallow marshes. There are four types of lechwe, and very few people have ever collected all four types before, so I am out to get the fourth one, and then they are all headed to a museum. These animals live in the water and die in the water. They never leave the marshes. So, it's hard to get to the lechwes because you have to wade in muck up to your knees.

So, we are riding from our successful hunt in Zambia, in David Ommoney's Jeep where there are all these civil wars. We get stopped by the border control and they are all drunk as hoot-owls. They have Russian machine gun pistols.

My proper Englishman hunting guide talks to them in their native language and tells me, "We have a bit of a problem. They want the lechwe."

I tell him to tell them, "We will not give you the animal."

He puts a gun to Sheila's head in the back of the car and said,

translated through David, "I will kill her unless you give us the animal."

I tell David to tell them, "I am on my honeymoon and she is lousy in bed and I would appreciate it if they would shoot her and take her off my hands."

With that, they fall down on the ground laughing hysterically.

We skinned the animal and gave them the meat, which is what they wanted anyway.

David said that it was very clever to use humor because they would have killed all of us.

Sheila didn't talk to me for days.

Sandy and Sheila Dann on their Honeymoon in Zambia with a lechwe, which are born and die in the water. Sandy collected all four types of lechwes, and they are now in a museum in Decatur, Georgia.

Along with the lechwe, Sandy and Sheila brought home many trophies. Sheila declared, "I didn't know we had walls for the first few
years of our marraige."

Sheila noted her mother was not a good speller and her legal name
is Shelia, but she preferred the spelling of Sheila for the book.

Picture yourself in Africa. In the northern part of Africa, most of them are Muslims, and little people like pygmies. In the south, they had only two years without a civil war with Muslims and natives. They have no compassion or sympathy. They do not understand these things. They have no words for sympathy. It would break my heart to watch. The women do all the work, to prepare meals and take care of children, and carry the water for the men and the men do nothing.

In the camps, they would create a wall of thorns to surround the camp maybe five-feet tall with a makeshift gate. A leopard could still jump over the wall, but it would keep most things out. The filth and brutality of women is horrible. I was there one time when an older woman was put out for the lions to eat her because she was old. It's hard for caring people to understand. Women are like cattle, not in all, but in many places in Africa.

So, this mindset made the humor work for the border control, and we lived.

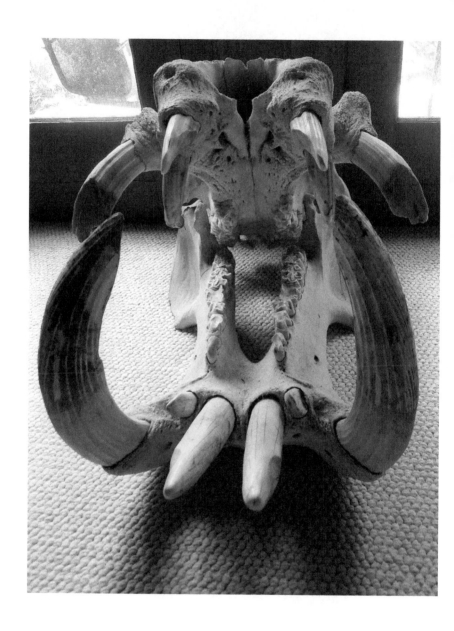

Our hunting guide, David Ommoney, asks if we would like a chance to shoot a world class hippo. Even though he's a grass eater, hippos kill more Africans than other animals. They don't eat people, but they can defend themselves and their big tusks can cut a person in two in one bite. They are normally very shy. There was a group of 50 of them that got caught in a pond and didn't migrate to the next watering hole. So, 50 are piled up and I ask, "Which one should I shoot?"

David responded, "They will decide."

He parked the Jeep out 100 feet from the pond, and presumably, had a back up gun ready to have our back, but we were never really sure of that. The animals were going crazy and we walk out 50 yards. One charges us, and Sheila is taking pictures. I tell her to just keep taking pictures, that "I need it to get closer so I can shoot this guy in the brain."

They can run at 40 miles-per-hour, and he's coming at us fast, so I have just one shot. Sheila is shaking so the photos are a little blurry. So, the shoot goes down and it looks like a truck hitting the water. This was the moment of truth.

A croc came up to get a piece of the 13 foot hippo while the spear-chuckers were cutting up the hippo. We killed the crocodile with one brain shot.

We wanted the skull of the hippo, not the meat. David hung the hippo carcass legs on a tree 40 feet away. Two guides built a honeymoon tree house for us to spend the night and have a grand view of the lions and meat eaters come out for dinner. We had a wonderful two bottles of local wine in a tree house 20 feet up. All was well until a lion tried to climb up the steps to get to us. His mistake. Danger was always near, and so was my gun to defend against danger.

We survived the hippo attack but in two seconds, we could have been dead.

Sandy was experienced at hunting Bongo and believed them to be among the most beautiful of the exotic animals. Above is a trophy in his home and right is a trophy from another safari.

CHAPTER 24,
SCRAPES WITH SCARY SAVAGES IN CENTRAL AFRICAN REPUBLIC

There were a few really scary trips. I had forgotten them until Sheila reminded me of them. It was truly as close to death as I have ever come. I was stuck in desolate darkness as Civil Wars were declared.

I went with a friend and his daughter to Paris, then to Africa. The idea was to go along because his wife was too terrified to go. Jim Harrison and his wife Donna planned the trip to the remote country in the Congo in Southwest Africa near the Calihari Desert. CAR, or the Central African Republic, was controlled at the time by the Foreign Legion, which kept them from having civil wars with each other. A lot of oil and minerals were in these countries, so they were under the control of the French.

The rarest, most valuable and most beautiful of all of the animals, the bongo, lived in this area. They only live in two places in the world. They travel around eating the tops of trees. They are pigs!

Sandy has in his home beautiful art objects made in CAR by the natives of alligator teeth and rare wood.

You can tell where they have been. They take their horns and push down trees and only eat a few of the tender branches at the tops of the trees. They travel ten to twenty miles a day in the deepest and darkest jungles of the world. They live in Kenya in the high mountain jungles, but most of the animals are extinct. Only 20 are left in the world, and they are in the CAR controlled by savages.

So, we go to CAR with the idea that Jim Harrison will collect a bongo. We landed in one of the two planes with 20 passengers that landed two times a week on a small runway. The Foreign Legion escorted us as we viewed the little city, which was the capital. We spent the night in the neat old French hotel, with all of 12 rooms, the largest in the whole capital city. The capital lies where the Nile separates.

We found beautiful art objects there made by the natives of alligator teeth and rare wood impervious to anything.

With our professional hunter Robin Hurt, we landed on the strip, then we got in his Jeep. He had cut 150 miles of road through the hinterlands. To tell you how thick the jungle is there, the path would be grown over in just two to three days. It was the true heart of darkness right out of the book with the same name by Joseph Conrad. Most of the natives there had never seen a white man. In three weeks there, we saw all of ten animals. The trees there were impenetrable. All of life is up in the trees. On the ground, you rarely see the sun, just tree trunks.

We found a wetland and baited up for the bongo and several other collectible animals did show up. We wandered off hunting while the natives built a platform and steps for us in a big tree on the edge of the marsh. The top was some 150 feet off the ground, which is like a 14 story building; it was high. Imagine climbing up little steps nailed together or tied together. Needless to say, sleeping quarters on just a tiny platform were challenging. All of us slept there, the guide, one assistant, the hunter and myself. Unbeknownst to me, I had trouble with me. I always kept bite size small sweets with me. I kept the goodies in the pocket of my vest.

Well, this is the land where the soldier ants lived. You have to be very careful of soldier ants walking around because they build a bridge with their bodies and can get anywhere. They are huge two-inch ants with small males, female queens and huge soldier ants as protectors. When animals are killed in the jungle, the ants can eat entire animal in no time. They consume the whole thing. They can eat an elephant just like that. They continually move seeking carcasses. They take huge bites leaving big holes in flesh.

Well, the ants smelled the candy. And the ants climbed up to the platform. They made a chain and climbed up all 150 feet. They started biting big chunks out of me. I was so wounded the next day, I was trying to be still to see the animals coming but it was hard. I stumbled back to camp with no sleep and walking in the stream, I hit a log with my shin and broke the skin not thinking anything of it. That night, I woke up and looked just below my kneecap at my leg bone. The ants had eaten my flesh.

Fortunately, I had a heavy duty medical kit which had been prepared by professional hunters who had been there. So, my days of following the hunt were over. I stayed in camp doctoring my wound and trying to prevent amputation. Fortunately my medications worked and I survived with two legs instead of just one.

I did not get to follow the tracking of the bongo but Jim did succeed. I healed enough to walk. When we drove back 50 miles to the runway our guide had cut in the thick jungle terrain, we waited for the plane but it never showed up. So, we had to head back through jungles being stopped many times by drunk border patrols. Our guide always kept pistols cocked and pointed at any border patrol people. The gun and silver dollars got us through 200 miles back to the capital. Now while arriving there, the police hit our car and demanded our valuables. All the beautiful streetlights and Colonial built buildings all were completely destroyed. The whole city had completely returned to the savages and the Foreign Legion was gone. The little hotel with 20 Europeans heavily armed were protecting themselves and waiting for the plane that was to come get them from the place that 45 days later would no longer be called a city.

We had numerous bad experiences if we tried to go outside of the hotel. We saw severe and brutal encounters where people were savagely killed for reasons we could not understand. The savages do not value human life. The guy who took me on the trip finally bribed our way on the plane, which landed three days later. It took 50 people out of the terror. Fortunately Jim had enough money to get us aboard.

See why I forgot this trip? I simply went to take photos and be a bodyguard. I wasn't the hunter on this trip. I have a few other trips I had forgotten as well.

Thankfully most of the safaris were enjoyable and interesting, so I would contine to return.

CHAPTER 25,
TERRIFYING MUSLIM ATTACKS IN SOUTHERN SUDAN WITH ROBIN HURT

It cost $11,000 to go on my first safari. Now a one month trip to Africa would cost $100,000. Eventually, I couldn't afford to hunt there.

The first time the Sudan was open to hunting in 20 years, I went. It's the largest country in Africa where the oil is now. It's south of Egypt and the Nile River goes through it. The Nile is the longest largest river in the world. The northern area is controlled by Muslims and the southern part is controlled by primitive natives. There is always fighting and wars between the two groups. So, while we were there hunting bongos, a civil war broke out.

The Sudan had not been open to hunting because of the wars in 20 years. When the north and south declared peace between the Muslims and natives, Robin Hurt got permission to hunt there in southern Sudan. I waited a year to get in with Robin Hurt because I wanted to hunt with him personally.

So we arrive and are hunting bongos. Remember that the bongos travel 20 miles a night and sleep during the day. They take the trees and knock them down with their horns and when the tree falls, they nibble only on the tender parts of the tops of trees then move on. So, it's easy to track them, you just look for downed trees. They cover such a huge amount of territory in a single evening meandering around, that is the tricky part.

One of our trackers got on the trail of a large male and we finally corralled him after a four day tracking.

At the same time, we ran into a Muslim hunting camp. The Muslims were killing everything in sight with automatic weapons and sending the meat back to northern Sudan on mules. They came far into the land of the southern Sudan natives. It would be like if Mexicans travelled all through the U.S. up to the border of Canada to poach animals, that is how far they had come.

As Robin Hurt was cleaning the camp, natives came and said that Muslims were killing the natives, too. Robin Hurt said he would close camp and I had to leave. So, Robin Hurt and his crew went into a Muslim camp at night and there were 20 Muslims who never saw the light of day again. As this was happening, I was in the Nile basin flood plane hunting.

So, he sent me on a two day Jeep trip on old roads where the British once had great mahogany tree farms, now all grown over. I was going to Khartoom in the middle of the country. I was going to where the runway was for the plane to pick me up and fly me back to Nairobi. In the meantime, we were hunting game that existed in that part of the world because it would be several weeks before a plane could pick me up. As we move cross country 500 miles on a reasonable road built by the British, we saw deserted guard stations every 50 miles that formerly stationed military personnel and groceries. The British were gone. Now the stations had no roofs and huge trees towered 30 feet high living inside the stations.

Robin Hurt killed over 1,000 elephants.
He had a deep attachment to Africa
including all of it's plants, animals and people.

So, we got closer to our destination and were on a flood plane, in a marsh on the flats of the Nile. Here we got the third little antelope like rare animal, the Nile lechwe.

I was taking a break and eating something and across on the horizon there were guys throwing spears at animals. I was peeling eggs and not paying attention.

David Ommoney got my attention and said, "They are getting ready to spear you and kill you unless you give them the lechwe."

I told him we could negotiate and I'd like to go to their camp to take photos. The natives move with their cattle as the waters of the Nile rise and fall. I didn't get killed but walked away after doing some trading for spears. The spears are all decorated and some are very thin and all are for hunting different animals.

The spears of southern Sudan were very thin as opposed to those of the Masai, which are very thick and heavy. The burn mark on their foreheads is the symbol of their tribe.

I went into the camp with a guide and interpreter, this naked guy, who was telling the chief that I brought them six dead animals to eat. My guide carried a "knob carry" which is a weapon the size of a baseball bat. I had a camera with me and they allowed me to take photos. They had not seen a white person before.

This is my negotiation of the deal. See the bands of ivory on their arms. They put them on when they are young and the arm grows around the band so they can never take it off.

There was a woman who was excommunicated and thrown out of the tribe. She was isolated for having a illegitimate child. The dirt and mud on their skin is to keep the bugs off.

Their tribe had pottery makers and basket weavers and spear makers. They are very primitive people.

Back near the Nile, we got the last plane out. I went back to Florida to resume a two year break while the fighting continued in the Sudan. I had to let these things go.

These were not my favorite trips.

CHAPTER 26,
LION HUNTING IN SOUTH AFRICA IN NAMBIA WITH JOHN LAWRENCE

On another trip, we went to the tip of South Africa in Nambia with the greatest professional lion hunter of all time, John Lawrence. My hunting guide David Ommoney said in his very perfect English, "Sandy, you need to hunt with the greatest lion hunter."

Nambia is a desert like country where the last of the pygmies live. They are three-feet tall full grown. They are humans left over from mankinds' roots millions of years ago. It took me a year for David to book me on a trip with John Lawrence and himself.

David warned me, "Lions in the desert are different. They will always come for you."

I arrived there and on the way looked out of the plane and saw my gun case fall out and hit the ground. It was heavily padded and seemed to still shoot well. Unbeknownst to me, the scope when riding in jeeps had been damaged. I would therefore be off on my shot and erratic so missed my first four animals that I was shooting to build my confidence with John Lawrence. But they were misses. This is serious when you are hunting animals that you know are coming to kill you. John Lawrence took my gun away and gave me one of his, which we zeroed in for me. I had no problems after that.

I enjoyed John's lion stories and experiences, however, I was concerned about his continuous drinking.

The young pygmies in that part of the world where mankind began, made me look like a giant at five-foot-six-inches. These are the most primitive of all the people in the world. They are also the greatest trackers in the desert like conditions where we were hunting.

Having shot a lot of animals for camp food, we were ready. John Lawrence thought I was ready to try for the big lion. We tracked for ten days until we finally got on the trail of a monster. Shortly after dawn, the trackers noses were close to the ground much like hunting dogs and they stopped in their tracks. John said, "The lion is close by."

We only took a dozen steps before the lion stood up about 100 feet away. He had been feeding on a kill. I sighted him and shot at the same time as John Lawrence shot which almost deafened my ear. It was totally unacceptable. I had paid a lot of money to be there to shoot the lion. I had the lion. I shot him. I didn't need him to shoot. When we got to the lion, both bullets were a few inches apart in the heart shot.

I was very angry and asked John for an explanation. He turned and said, "I will tell you why later." Back at camp over two martinis, John told me his story. Two months before I arrived, the lion got through and killed John's best tracker he had for over 12 years. A month before I arrived, a lion got through and killed John's client.

John said, "I realized then, the lions were coming for me because I had lost my nerve. They can feel the fear. You are my last client and I will never hunt again."

It was so traumatic that I forgot that story. Back then I wasn't afraid. John had lost his courage. When I first started hunting, I remember David Ommoney training me, "You must never let the animals know you are afraid. They can sense this."

Killers go after the one in fear because they know they will stand in fright and not fight back. To think this was the greatest lion hunter of the time and I was his last client. I always wondered, "why me?"

Later it would happen to me and I myself would have a reason to stop hunting.

Sandy Dann with spear and shield he bartered with Masai warrior
in Kenya.

On my third trip to Kenya with David Ommoney, we were hunting a leopard. David was a great hunter. He was part of an old family in England that left to run the countries of Kenya and Tanzania. The British were trying to control the riches of the countries, the gold and silver and the animals. During the Mau Mau uprising from 1952 to 1960 in Kenya between the rebels and the British army, David was dispatched with 51 family members and people loyal to his family. They went up to Mount Kenya, which is both on the equator and snow covered, so that tells you how high it is. By the time he was 21-years-old, he had killed 20 Masai. He grew up in that part of the world and loved it, so he made a world-class hunting guide.

We found a leopard that was in his final days of living in the throes of death. You can see from his skull that he was missing teeth and would have a hard time killing and eating. He was bright because he was ancient. We would put bait out for him and build a stand and he would come and poop in our stand at night to let us know that he knew we were there.

We were hunting in a marsh between two hills. David Ommoney sees the leopard sitting on a big rock watching to see if we are coming. To get to the leopard, we could see him half a mile across the marsh, but we would have to drive 15 miles around. The leopard would see and hear the hunting buggy and would hide. He was smart. If he heard the buggy, he wouldn't get the bait.

So, to outsmart him, we wake up at 3 a.m. and drove to the blind so he doesn't hear the hunting buggy in his morning walk. Needless to say, walking in the dark with elephants and lions all around us was terrifying. We got safely into the blind and at dawn he came out to eat. We shot him.

After he was skinned, the Masai pulled him out from under the skinner's head at night. The Masai stole my leopard skin. They are so clever, they took it right from under the head of the native while he was sleeping.

David Ommoney went to the chief and demanded that the skin be returned and gave him a time frame. When he was not returned that evening, David Ommoney took one of their bulls. Animals are money to the Masai. He roped the bull and drug him to the camp and staked him outside his tent. Three days went by with no return of the leopard skin.

In the meantime, we were hunting other game and when we came in for breaks in the middle of the day, I'd do a mile and a half run out of the camp to stay in shape. One day we might sit still in a stand all morning and the next day we might climb cliffs all day, so I had to stay in shape to keep up. Some 20 Masai natives would circle me carrying heavy spears and shields as I ran each day. They wore no shoes but had one inch thick calluses to protect their feet from the severe thorns. I should have been afraid but I wasn't.

The moment of truth was coming and we were ready to pack up camp and leave and execute the bull. The leopard skin was returned.

During my runs, I admired one of the Masai's shields. It is a 40 pound shield made from impervious wood that even a bullet cannot get through. The spear is heavy also and strong and the Masai can throw it half the length of a football field and hit a glass. As we were packing, I got one of my semi-interpreters who spoke the Masai tongue and I speaking Swahili of the pygmies to negotiate the purchase of his shield and spear. I was surprised that after bickering, he wanted U.S. dollars, and we agreed upon $200. I was given the shield and spear and he the dollars. As he was walking away, he stopped and in perfect English in a British accent said, "I say there, you Americans are awfully chincy."

I was flabbergasted. In great surprise, I asked, "You speak English?"

He responded, "I should. I went to Oxford."

I shouted back, "What are you running around here living like this?"

He said, "If you live like a Masai for one night, you would understand."

I found out later he was their physician and teacher. His father was the head of the tribe and had 14 wives and quite a few of them went to Oxford.

There are always surprises on safaris, some scary and others simply interesting.

CHAPTER 28,
WAVE THROUGH HOPE TOWN HOUSE IN 1999

The Hope Town, Bahamas house that endured category four and a half Hurricane Floyd above before and after the hurricane.

Hurricane Floyd gave us a shock as we first saw the house on the cover of the *Miami Herald* which showed the house sitting in the ocean. Our home in Hope Town in the Abacos, in the Bahamas, was built by the same people who build boats in Man-O-War Cay. A 40 foot wave went over the house during category 4-and-a-half Hurricane Floyd. This is before and after the storm. We had a lot of adventures in the Bahamas.

We kept a Bandit boat there (photo on page 51) that we got in Palm Beach where they built five hulls. They were double hulled so they won't leak if you hit a reef. It's 12-feet wide. It has outboards and platforms on the back. We added two sleeping places in the front and one in the middle. There are places to store your gear under the seats. It has a double tower and you can steer in the tower if you want.
There was one time fishing on this boat when a 70 pound barracuda jumped right in the boat. From 50 feet out he flew through the boat and smashed into the steering column. You never know when fishing what will happen.

CHAPTER 29,
SANDY'S LAST BIG GAME HUNT IN 2001

We spent a lot of time at our ranch in Volusia County, Florida. The ranch has 1,000 acres and a nice house, little but nice. It's a two bedroom with three twenty-foot porches all the way around, with beds around to sleep outside on the screened-in porches. It has cathedral ceilings with pecky cypress, and all the fine details of a cracker home. I hunted there with family and friends. I also hunted for 48 years at a hunting camp on Deseret Ranch for deer and turkey.

As a big time game hunter, I went on 15 safaris, with 3 trips to Mongolia and Russia, the last one to Kazakhstan. I've hunted in most countries in South America, plus Canada, and Alaska here in the U.S.

I was always guided by the great hunters, who preached to never make an animal suffer. If you wounded an animal, it's your responsibility to hunt him down and put him out of his misery. I've had to track animals in Africa, one was for a day-and-a-half, to put one wounded animal to rest. My hunting guide, David Ommoney, one of the greatest hunters of all time, made sure for me to learn this, that animals are not to be punished with pain.

The hurricane damage to the Bahamas house had been taking me away from hunting on the Deseret Farm, where this year they decided to have a black powder season. You use black powder guns like in the Civil War where you stuff your gunpowder and pack down the shell; it's a one shot type of deal. Having no particular experience with that but wanting to hunt, on the last day of black powder season, I finally got to the ranch to try out my black powder gun.

An hour before dawn, I walked down Three Mile Road to and an old railroad tram. Within a few hundred yards of the tram, I noticed a ladder tree stand overlooking the wetlands. This is normally a pasture but with Hurricane Floyd, the pastures were knee-deep in water. I loaded my black powder gun and climbed up the ladder to a seat on a branch. I figured if someone went to the trouble to build a big stand, there must be a big buck in the area. So, I tried to imitate a fight between two bucks, as this was the time of year where bucks establish their territory. So, I got my boots on the top of the ladder and started pounding and breaking branches to imitate a fight with the vibrations on the ground of two fighting bucks. This sound and vibration would drive off every deer but the big boy. Soon after the first light, my imitation was rewarded by seeing a deer coming through palmettos and hitting the big wet pasture with water two-feet deep. He looked like a big motorboat coming.

By the time I get my pre-loaded gun up, the deer was standing 20 paces away in water looking for his competitors. I fired my black powder gun and when the smoke disappeared, I could only see one horn sticking out of the water. I climbed down and waded out, making mistake number one. I hadn't reloaded, which meant the black powder and the whole nine yards, which takes time. As a professional hunter, you know not to approach an animal without a loaded gun.

Mistake number two is I go down with the gun strapped to my back. I see the horns under water and bend down to lift the deer up. He stood up and flipped me backwards. Who knows where the gun went? When he stood up, I was looking at a really pissed off ten-point deer, with no weapon. The deer tried to move but collapsed and went back under. I realized I had a spine shot and had paralyzed his back and legs so he couldn't move. The deer would try to make a step and went back under.

I pulled out my Randall Knife with the idea of stabbing him. I stabbed him in what I thought was the juggler. Evidently, it was not the juggler as the next thing I know, I am sailing through the air and the knife is gone.

Now, I have no means to dispatch the deer. So, as he goes back down again, I got behind him and I figured I could hold his horns, and put my head between his horns and push him under the water and drown him. So, that is what I did. I got behind the deer, grabbed him with both horns so I could hold him under the water. The deer rolled his eyes back. Our eyes were a few inches apart. Then he collapsed and went back under, then back up. Then he started crying. This went on for 20 minutes until it was finally over.

I realized at age 69, I had made all the mistakes I had been taught not to make. At age 69, it was time to quit big game hunting. It was my last game hunt. I am still a bird shooter but not a game hunter.

There are 42 animals in a museum outside of Atlanta. I said goodbye to them. Most all the animals are record class. I hunted for the best of the best. It might take years to look at thousands of animals before I shot the big boy.

Most all of them have a museum mount. Look at the plastic under the skin for the structure of the jaw and the teeth, and the wrinkles. You still see the blood vessels and the chest muscles. The plastic model is of that specific animal.

The cape buffalo is never to be tamed by man. If you get near him, you would just get killed by him. He's mean, mean, mean, mean. They run in herds, so there are a thousand coming at you. You just hide wherever you can and get away from them. He's a scary piece of equipment. He has a mean and scary look because he is mean.

"As a big time game hunter, I went on 15 safaris ... I realized at age 69, I had made all the mistakes I had been taught not to make. It was time to quit big game hunting. It was my last game hunt."

SECTION 3:
SANDY DANN'S LEGACY OF ADVENTURE STORIES
AS TOLD THROUGH OTHERS

Writer's Note: The legacy of a storyteller by nature is to have the stories retold. Two additions here are made by Sandy's wife of 30 years Sheila, and his oldest daughter Carol. You can feel the humor and lighthearted energy of Sandy himself in the words, gestures, and smiles of the tales. Each person finishes each other's sentences and adds details or a punchline. Friends take on the voice of the comedian as they tell a "Sandy story," too. Loved ones and dear friends throughout Orlando, and across the globe, retell Sandy's stories always with a laugh remembered.

Sandy's oldest daughter Carol and wife Sheila at El Saladero Ranch in Uruguay. They tell "Sandy stories" with similar gestures and punchlines. Sandy stories always have a punch line!

CHAPTER 30,
SANDY'S WIFE SHEILA AND BAHAMAS SHARKS

I fought off sharks for him. That's why he married me. We dated for four years and were in the Bahamas in the Abacos off Scotland Cay. It's always sharky. We anchored Bandit, a 35 foot boat inside the reef and swam over the reef to the outside to 20 to 30 foot freediving in holes in the reef. In there, we found some nice groupers which we had on a hand line. Unfortunately the blood in the water attracted a bull shark. I see the shark coming after him because Sandy is down in a hole after a grouper and all you see is these feet dangling out of the hole. I dive down there with a speargun Sandy made charging and hitting the shark to get off Sandy. So, Sandy backs out and a bull shark is after us. We swim up into two feet of water with reefs under us and waves crashing on us, and we get all cut up on the razor sharp reef. The shark kept coming after us so I hit him twice with the tip of the spear without the spear tip. He still followed us back to the boat.

SHEILA AND SKIING BIG SKY, MONTANA
Another time in Big Sky Montana, with Carl and Sandy, we went up two levels on a ski lift. I crawled and looked over the ledge and said, "no!" It was a category five straight down with rocks. I don't get scared easily but it was scary and horrible. I sat there with Carl till someone came and rescued us. I got back down on the lift.

It's always fun with Sandy. Every day is an adventure. Every time we would leave for a trip, my staff would want to know where we were going and if I'd come back alive.

CHAPTER 31,
SANDY'S DAUGHTER CAROL

CAROL IN TREE STANDS AT THE RANCH
Everybody did the same, girls and boys. At o-dark-thirty, we'd be up in tree stands with guns slung over our shoulders in tree stands three to four stories tall. We'd hike up in those tree stands on the 40 square mile ranch. Thinking about it gives me the heebie jeebies. The stands are just one foot by one foot, and might be rotting wood that had been there a few years. I have a fear of heights, so I'd be breathing so hard getting up there and would just sit down and hug my tree. Us kids would get together and make a pact with each other so we could take turns sleeping. One would stay up to watch for dad coming from the blind, or if we saw a turkey or doe by the trees. We were all 8, 9, 10, 11-years-old. I was the oldest, so if anything happened, I was to get everyone out.

I was 25-years-old and 8 months pregnant and at o-dark-thirty, I was up in a tree with a deer coming. I went to the hospital after that and had my son.

CAROL MONKEY-ING IN AFRICA
In Africa, the lions roar so loudly that it echoes. A lion and four cubs killed a zebra and they fed on it for three days, just 100 yards away from our tents. They eat 50 to 75 pounds at one time then they are all spread out with blood all over gorged. Then the hyenas come in and howl all night. You can't imagine how loud it is. We have Maasai walking around protecting us and we have these little flashlights. I was rooming with Yvonne and we agreed to wake each other if we needed to go to the bathroom tent at night. So, we walk out in the pitch black and see the huge eyes of a bush monkey hanging from a tree and scream at the top of our lungs. We woke up dad and everyone else with the screaming and laughing hysterically.

CAROL IN VERO BEACH WITH SHARK

Another adventure at the crack of sunlight in Vero Beach, a tenacious bull shark kept coming at the propeller until we cut his face. Off our Vero Beach hotel in a 13 foot 6 inch Boston Whaler, we filled the well in the back of the boat with salt water to keep live bait fish. We went 13 miles straight off the hotel to the 60 foot reef where fish congregated. Instantaneously we had a bite with a 50 pound goliath grouper. We would be out and back loaded with fish by 9 a.m. before people from Sebastian or Jupiter Inlets got out there. Well, the fish and blood was draining from the back of the boat, and this bull shark, which is the worst of all, has decided the propeller is a wounded fish. He wouldn't let up and kept attacking the boat. We turned on the propeller and cut his face off.

Our dad taught us that after spearing fish, you get back in the boat and move because the blood and vibrations of a sick injured fish attract sharks, or men in gray. He taught us how to fish and hunt and be safe.

CAROL AND SANDY DANN THE TURD IN THE BAHAMAS

My dad and his sister Joanie and her husband and a few other people had tanks and spear guns in the Bahamas. We each shot one lobster. Then we had the tanks to teach Pam to dive because she had a new license.

The Bahamian authorities jumped in the boat and searched it and all the gear. There is always tension between the natives and the outsiders like us, even though we have a home there. They took us to land and locked us in a room the size of the couch. It was 105 degrees and the room smelled like throw up and poop.

Dad said, "Let me out and I'll go to the bank to get our bail."

He knew the girl at the bank so we get money and they are going to try us the next day. So, we are at the trial and the judge has on full white robe, and they have all our gear they absconded with there. We explain that we each got one lobster, which is legal.

Sometimes you can't understand the Bahamians because the way they talk with British and Bahamian accents. The Bahamas have only been independent from Britain 40 years. So, the judge says with his heavy accent, "I'm going to fine you two-thousand-dollars and keep the gear, and the kids can go, but now you Carl Dann the Turd ..."

He meant to say "third" but it came out "turd" and the more he tried to get order in his court, the more we were laughing and rolling on the floor hysterically, insulting the judge. We still laugh about our dad, "Carl Dann the Turd."

We have heard all of the stories in our lifetimes so many times but we still can't remember them all. Our dad is all about humor and adventure.

The humorous delivery of Sandy Dann tales of dreadful errors in judgment, clearly are in the safe hands of the Dann family.

CHAPTER 32,
SANDY'S FRIENDS SHARE A LAUGH
CAPTAIN PHIL WOODS (submitted in writing for this book)

My parents shipped me off to a fancy boy's prep school in 1948, The Hill School in Pennsylvania. During my second and third year, I roomed with a nice young athletic guy named Lamar Hunt from Dallas and we became close friends. We graduated from The Hill in 1951. Lamar went to SMU and I to UNC at Chapel Hill where I joined the Phi Delta Theta fraternity along with Carl "Sandy" Dann from Orlando and 15 or 20 other pledges.

After graduation from UNC in 1955, I joined the Marine Corps and was stationed in Quantico, Virginia, where I met my wife Dodie Mitchell from D.C. We were married in 1957 and Lamar, Sandy and other dear friends and school buddies were in the wedding.

Now Sandy had driven his dilapidated car from Chapel Hill to D.C. for the wedding and he volunteered to go to the airport and pick up Lamar and his wife. Lamar was the son of H.L. Hunt from Dallas, at that time the largest independent oil producer in the world and reportedly the wealthiest man on the planet, worth over two billion bucks, in 1957!

But I digress, Sandy went to the airport to pick up the Hunts who had arrived in the corporate plane. Sandy's car was so rusted out, you could lift the floor mats and see the highway passing below. They made it safely back to the hotel and Dodie and I got married the next day.

Following a spectacular reception, most of the wedding party adjourned to the Washington estate of Mr. John Archbold, who was Dodie's godfather. The party went on for hours with numerous fully clothed bridesmaids an groomsmen performing cannon balls into the pool.

Somewhere along the wee hours (Dodie and I had long gone to catch a plane,) Sandy, John McWhirter, Frank Jackson, Dan Bellinger and a couple of other groomsmen from Tampa decided to take a tour of Washington in Sandy's car. They drove halfway up the steps of the Lincoln Memorial. They got out and climbed up and were sitting in Lincoln's lap enjoying another cocktail when the police arrived. Nobody went to jail. It was 1957. I'm glad I missed that one!

SECTION 4: A COLLECTION OF PHOTOS AND SMILES

Sandy Dann hunted and fished in rugged terrain over much of the world. Not all of his adventures were life threatening. Some were just plain fun! Shown here are friends on a hunt in Canada.

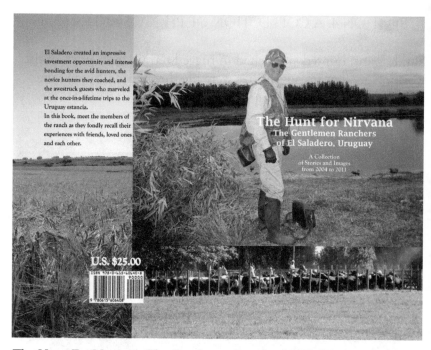

The Hunt For Nirvana, The Gentlemen Ranchers of El Saladero, Uruguay, A Collection of Stories and Images from 2004 to 2011, was dedicated to Sandy and Sheila Dann by their partners in the estancia. You can buy it on www.Amazon.com or www.BN.com. These are a few of Sandy's photos of Uruguay not included in that book.

This is my favorite photo of El Saladero. These two trees grew together and one is choking the other tree out. This is where we would meet after hunts to tell our stories. I really miss that place.

Sandy hunting at the pond on his Florida ranch with his Jack Russell companion Laddie. In 2012, the Danns added a pair of Jack Russell puppies to their long list of canine pets, named after Bonnie and Clyde, the hunting dogs at El Saladero estancia.

Sandy is a much sought after fishing and hunting buddy among Florida's outdoor enthusiasts. With his extensive experience and enthusiasm, the probability of a big catch or big kill is greatly enhanced. Literally no mountain is too high.

The face of the Heart of Darkness in Africa was photographed by Sandy Dann on one of his 15 safaris.

Sandy and Sheila enjoying a post-hunt cocktail and kiss in Scotland.

Lives are measured not in the things we collect in a vessel, but that which we leave behind. Sandy Dann has inspired and positively influenced people of all ages and cultures in many places on safaris and sailing adventures around the world.

Through both education and intuition, Sandy Dann stayed alive to experience adventures around the globe and return to tell the tales. In each precarious situation, he applied the teachings from both mentoring grandfathers who inspired him. He made life better for the people and places he touched. He has created a legacy of extraordinary compassion and affinity for all the things of the earth.

Sandy, Sheila and "all the litte indians" as he affectionately refers to his children and grandchildren at the Dann family home by Dubsdread Golf Course in Orlando.

Sandy's favorite Mongolian desert flower he photographed as much as he did the grand expanse of the desert and the coveted hunted trophies. The iconic Mongolian desert scene on the cover of this book was among Sandy's favorite photos.

CPSIA information can be obtained at www.ICGtesting.com
Printed in the USA
LVOW02*1234200814

399814LV00001B/1/P